Women and Their Emotions

Women and Their Emotions

by
Miriam Neff

MOODY PRESS
CHICAGO

ISBN:0-8024-5151-9

4 5 6 7 Printing/GB/Year 87 86 85 84
Printed in the United States of America

Dedicated to the greatest expanders of my emotions . . .

our children

Valerie
John
Charles
Robby

Contents

Preface: A Woman's Perspective

Why another book on emotions? I have had to answer that question in women's seminars, in church pulpits, and on radio interviews. I have a nice pat public answer. Most of the books written on emotions have been written by men. I think there's something to be gained from a woman's perspective on our emotions. I see the world through a woman's eyes; I feel with a woman's feelings. It's possible that our feelings are more intense. Twice as many women as men are depressed. Women seek professional help regarding their emotions more frequently than men do, and we are more susceptible to mood changes.

Emotions are good and God-given. Not enough emphasis has been placed on the positives of our feelings. We agree that the bumper sticker saying, "If it feels good, do it," is a fool's yardstick. But suppressing our feelings and living like robots with the emotional blahs doesn't honor God either.

A friend once told me that I am piggy on life and a glutton on living. So be it. I want to feel, enjoy, and use to the fullest everything God has created in me—emotions included. Nice public answers were enough to make me dive into the water, in dealing with my emotions, but I needed a greater motivation when I faced the octopus of my own emotional struggles. As I sorted and searched for better answers, I faced tentacles in my own life as I never had before, like anger, depression, and grief.

In dealing with emotions, I have been both the counselor and the client. Most writers have written from the counselor's side of the desk. It is comfortable there. I know the feeling—degrees nicely framed on the wall, referral numbers by the phone, a comfortable chair for the client, and a box of tissues for the women.

The other side of the desk is a different world. Sitting in the client's chair, I was afraid my spiritual halo would be tarnished by the fact that I needed professional help. But some emotional tangles are too confusing and painful to sort alone. Professional help in the untangling process was only part of the solution. Emotional habits had to be broken. I had to choose to change. Though I prefer change to be instant, I will battle some old emotional habits all my life.

Battles are seldom fought alone; victories are sweeter when shared. Do you feel that you are the only person whose emotions feel like the strangling tentacles of an octopus? "No temptation has overtaken you but such as is common to [woman]" (1 Corinthians 10:13). (The original word for man is *anthropos*, which means male or female, and as I said earlier, I see through a woman's eyes.)

You are not alone. Emotions can be transformed to become both helpful and useful. The victory of changing those strangling tentacles into strong, helpful arms is sweet. I'd like to share it.

Acknowledgments

Special thanks to Ruth Beam, who gave me professional advice and questioned and inspired me in the process, as this manuscript became a book.

Two other key members of the team were my husband's parents—Father Neff, who applied his English-teacher eye to the product, and Mother, who typed and typed and typed!

Introduction

Emotions are a gift from God. Do you believe it? I confess that I sometimes wish I had no feelings. I'd rather be "blah," especially when the crowd is standing dry-eyed and indifferent as our national anthem is played at a game, and tears are streaming down my face. I picture our tattered flag still waving over an embattled colonial fort, a blood-stained flag flying over a divided blue and gray nation, an ignored flag flying over our industrialized, mushrooming, wealthy country—a nation that God in His sovereignty has chosen to preserve.

I've wished I had no feelings as I fumed in anger over Kool-Aid powder sprinkled over the floor or gum matted in the carpet. I'd like to live without the nausea of rejection from a key person in my life, or the aloneness and grief at seeing Mama's casket closed for the last time. Please color me *blah*. "Emotions?" I've asked. "A gift from God?"

Yes. If I accept the Bible as true—which I do—then the creation of emotions was God's doing. And He intended them for good. How do we bridge the gap between the good that God intended and what we often experience? The answer to that question would require at least an encyclopedia. But may I offer you this small paperback as the beginning?

I've heard it said that women are more in tune with their feelings and more sensitive than men. I'm not so sure about that. I am sure about one thing: we more frequently allow our emotions to lead us. While men are *thinking* about what should be done, we're sorting out how we *feel* about it. We're likely to act based on those feelings before we've applied our minds to the issue at hand. The marriage of our minds and our emotions equals what Scripture refers to as the heart. Bridging the gap is marrying the mind to the emotions and placing them both under God's control.

Let's explore how anger can be positive, why Christians experience depression, and what good can come of such feelings. Let's rediscover empathy and learn how to break bad emotional habits.

About our hearts: let's commit ourselves to the marriage of our emotions to our minds. May the words that Nehemiah said to the God of Abraham be true of us as well. "You found his heart faithful to you" (Nehemiah 9:8a, NIV*).

* *New International Version.*

1

Who's in Charge?

How do you capture an octopus? Do you grab one leg and tuck it under your arm, hoping the other seven tentacles don't strangle you before you capture another? Do you grab two legs in each hand and tie them together? What if the other four tentacles cover your eyes and trip you while you're tying the knot? Sound ridiculous? I think we sometimes wrestle with our emotions this way. We decide we must tackle one area, let's say, anger. We work at it for weeks. Maybe we even see some progress. But, meanwhile, we get jealous of someone who never has to wrestle with anger because he is such a docile person.

Maybe we decide we'll take loneliness and depression and deal with them in one grand program of activity. We're going to get involved in worthwhile projects; we're going to contact old friends and plan get-togethers; we're going to get our appearances back in shape. But in the bustle of activity we find insecurity stalking us, messing up or tangling our well-laid plans. (What if my old friends don't want to see me? What if the hospital turns down my application to volunteer? What if I can't lose weight?) It's hard to battle inadequacies, loneliness, and depression if insecurity has our hands tied behind our backs.

Where do we begin, then?

Act, realizing your emotions will react.

Susan was sixteen and pregnant. She had most of her life ahead of her. Her boyfriend had never intended to marry her; but for that matter, she didn't want to get married either—not now, anyway. The solution that would disrupt her life the least, she thought, was abortion. It was simple in a big city. Within five days the phone calls had been made, the check written, and the appointment kept; Susan was no longer pregnant. In the days that followed, Susan felt relief. Her parents never knew, so there were no scenes. She missed only a few days of school, so there were no incompletes. She and her boyfriend stopped seeing each other, but she knew she could handle that.

Susan believed that she had solved her problem. She had taken action, changed her circumstances, and everything was OK. She did not realize that her emotions would react. Little publicity is given to the fact that girls who have abortions experience periods of psychological trauma. I knew Susan. Having been her high school counselor and living in the same neighborhood, I saw her occasionally. Her first time of trauma came at the time her baby would have been born. Seeing babies at that time depressed her. When there were no babies around, she still struggled with guilt.

After her marriage, Susan gave birth for the first time. What might have been a time of exhilaration and marvel at the miracle of life and a time of deep inner joy became a gray time. She thought of another face that might have been.

Feminists and humanists say a woman should be able to have an abortion on request, because she is in control of her body and nothing else counts. But every woman, by God-instilled instinct, knows that when she becomes pregnant another life is involved. Susan had not made room for the fact that abortion would erase the thread of life yet introduce a tangle of emotions.

Action. It can stop. It can be changed. But we do not act with our emotions in neutral. Because each of us is an integrated whole, our emotions are geared to our behavior. Our emotions will respond to our actions—perhaps not now, or even tomorrow. We can predict some of our emotional reactions, but many of them will surprise us.

Sybil's experience was similar to Susan's. But Sybil decided to have her baby. At the time, her life was disrupted more than Susan's. But further down the line Sybil did not experience the emotional trauma that Susan did. She saw her baby. She knew he was healthy. She knew that he was adopted by people who wanted a child. There was room in their lives for this little person. He was desired and loved. Sybil knew she had done the unselfish thing. She had put aside what looked best at the moment for what was best for everyone, including herself, in the long run.

Why do we act without considering that our emotions will react? Popular psychology has tried to teach us that we are simple beings; we can learn and unlearn—forming and breaking habits. It's easiest to act based on what feels good now, what is convenient now, and what pleases another person now. It's harder to think of the future and the long-term effects of our actions. Most of us would have less guilt, frustration, loneliness, and insecurity if we were more thoughtful in our planning— instead of acting hastily and impulsively. We need to realize that our emotions cannot be separated from our actions.

Act based on fact.

Absolutes are unpopular today. Our situation ethics, our relativism, and our "if it feels good, do it" philosophy are all glaring results of our laying aside the truths of God's Word. Edith Schaeffer defines it in A Way of Seeing:

> But there is a pollution more to be feared than polluted beauty . . . the pollution of the absolute Word of God, the pollution of the Bible. Insidiously, there is a dangerous pollution going on, sometimes with delicate deception. . . . Phrases seem the same. Only a little is removed: a word there, a meaning somewhere else. This portion is deleted from history and changed into myth or parable. That portion is turned away from as unimportant, open to question. The early part of Genesis is treated with a shrug, and the reality of God's speaking in the epistles is dismissed with a phrase attributing what is being taught only to the man who is writing. Infallibility is a word that suddenly becomes an embarrassment.*

When we have internalized truths that we believe with our minds and our hearts, they function as the foundation for our actions. Our feelings affirm our choices. What happens when those truths are removed? Perhaps the foundation is not removed and thrown out. Perhaps its only cracked here and there, a

* Edith Schaeffer, A Way of Seeing (Old Tappan, N.J.: Revell, 1977).

chunk is taken out, a pile of "possibly's" are thrown over, making it hard to find one's footing. We no longer have a sure basis for acting.

Where do we go? We have no working truth as our guideline. We have no facts on which to base our lives. It is like standing on a beach as the tide comes in. It's like finding yourself in waves that at one point rocked you gently but now are getting rougher, enveloping you. What was an exciting gamble is becoming frightening. We flounder around to reach for something stable. At this point, since it is popular to believe there are no absolutes, we ought not to be surprised to find that people act based on feeling; facts have been discredited, and the foundation they once trusted has been made to appear faulty, as the foundation of truth, God's absolute, is hacked and chopped.

We have allowed the world's idea of God to creep into our own thinking. It is popular today to blame God for everything bad that humans can't control. For instance, on my insurance policy I see that tornadoes, earthquakes, damaging snowstorms, and trees falling on my house or car are "acts of God." Most likely we will blame God for bad circumstances.

But it is not God's intention for the humans He created in love to suffer. Look at Job's example. His children died; his financial empire toppled; his friends deserted him. Although his wife remained with him, she made his life miserable. To make matters worse, his body became covered with disease. Yet we read in Job 1:22: "Through all this Job did not sin nor did he blame God." It seems to me that there is foundational truth that is vital to the healthy expression of each emotion. Believing God's goodness makes all the difference in the world.

Usually our attempts to manage our emotions are based on changing circumstances, rather than on actions based on fact. Rarely is this successful for long—and no wonder. As one person, I cannot do much about many of the circumstances in my life. I can make choices and change *me*, but I can't change other people. I may be able to affect some events, but my power is limited.

How do we manage our feelings? We internalize God's foundational facts. This changes our behavior. Based on facts, I can choose to change. My feelings then mesh with what I believe and what I am doing. Emotions were never intended by God to be the basis for action. Action is to be determined by His absolute truth. In this light, our feelings add wealth to our actions.

"If it feels good, do it?" Hardly. There's a better way. "The mind of man plans his way but the LORD directs his steps" (Proverbs 16:9).

2

It's Good to Feel

Why do we feel, anyway? Why did God create us with emotions? Aren't there times when you wish you had no heart, that your head housed only a center for intellect? Then you wouldn't hurt, right? But the fact remains that, even if we deny that God put it there, we have a center in our head for feelings, for emotions. Secular humanism tells us we can separate our emotional center from our intellectual center. Science disagrees. So does the Bible. So does my experience—and yours too, no doubt.

What if we were granted our occasional wish that we had no feelings? What would happen? Besides not hurting, here's what would happen in my life. I couldn't cry with joy over red, wrinkled newborn babies. I couldn't cheer with excitement over touchdowns and pins at wrestling meets. I wouldn't be stirred by the swelling emotion in Franz Liszt's "Second Polonaise." My husband and I wouldn't squeal over our baby's first wobbly step, or swell with pride as our "child" steps forward and reaches for his diploma. I wouldn't take deep breaths as the sun rises over the ocean. I couldn't sense the tenderness and desire returned when my eyes lock with someone I love.

It's not that we don't ever want to feel. We'd just like to change how we feel when we are uncomfortable or in pain.

The world contains many hurts. Our children learn that before they learn to walk. One way we try to cope with all the hurt is by walling off our emotions. "If I don't allow myself to feel, I won't hurt," we reason. True. But there is a much better way. Not feeling reduces the hurt, but the shell that keeps the hurt out also keeps out the joy.

Walling off the emotions in your life can lead to headaches, ulcers, or drug dependency. Perhaps you will never encounter such serious problems. But there will be one sure result: you will be desensitized. People around you may hurt, but you won't notice. If you have refused to *feel*, you will not realize the hurts of others. In addition, your joys will not be real; like your hurts, they will be limited.

You won't see the sun clearly on a beautiful day. Looking out your window in the fall, you will simply see a square glass opening that probably needs cleaning. You could be viewing your very own panorama. You could be seeing greens mellowing into yellows, rusts, and crimson. You could be seeing moss-covered branches, punctuated by the stark black of old limbs.

You won't enjoy your children as much—or anything, for that matter. Not feeling may reduce the hurt, but life is likely to be, to put it simply, a bore. The biggest laughs and deepest joys will touch someone else's life, not yours. That is the price that desensitizing demands.

God had something good in mind when He made us with feelings. "I praise you because I am fearfully and wonderfully made; your works are wonderful, I know that full well" (Psalm 139:14, NIV). David knew God had made a good thing when He formed him. Perhaps you feel you are an "emotional" person. David certainly was. Tell the Lord that you know He made a good thing when He created you that way. Praise the Lord that you're a feeling person.

God loves you. This phrase is often spoken but seldom believed. "For God so loved the world . . ." Many people can imagine this only in a spiritualized sense. "God loves me because I love and have accepted His Son," they say. They imagine themselves in a throng of unworthy people crowded about Jesus, welcomed into God's presence because they are with the right Person. That's not the whole truth. There's something even greater than that.

God likes you. He likes me. The particular blend of personality characteristics He gave you is just right for Him to delight in. It is different from every other person in the world. And God likes you that way! Does this seem hard to grasp? It's the first step, and an absolutely necessary one in order to manage your emotions. A person who's apologizing for being alive can't get on with enjoying living. If I can't accept my emotional makeup, I certainly can't manage it.

Judy was an emotional woman. She cried when she found a bird with a broken wing. When her husband was late for dinner, she poured the spaghetti down the garbage disposal. She cheered wildly when her son ran out on the football field, but ranted and raved over his jacket left on the hallway floor. The phone rang one day. It was her daughter's high school counselor. Her daughter was in trouble. In the scene that followed that night, her daughter blurted out, "I can never talk to you. You can't listen, and you make a mountain out of a molehill. Let's face it, Mom. You can't cope."

Sobbing to her neighbor the next day, Judy said, "I just can't help it. I've always been this way. If I just weren't so emotional."

Judy had the potential for being a devoted, understanding mother. But she had focused her feelings on pleasing herself. Family members were to fit in with her plans and her schedule, or watch out! When her emotional intensity made her miserable, she tried to suppress her feelings. With her high energy level, she could have managed her household efficiently and been competent on a part-time or perhaps full-time job or accomplished much that was worthwhile. But she burned out lots of energy on tantrums and manipulating people to do things her way. She did not manage her emotions; they managed her. Inside she wished she weren't so emotional for a selfish reason—she thought her life would be easier.

Judy needed to grasp first of all that her particular personality blend—emotions and all—was good and God-created. The security of knowing that would begin to free her of manipulating others. Most manipulating tries to hoist a sign that says, "Please make me look like I am somebody special." When a person realizes that she is somebody special, she doesn't need to carry a sign saying so.

As Judy began to thank the Lord that He liked her, she found herself manipulating less and, as a matter of fact, life was easier not only for Judy, but for her family.

Judy could have tried the "I'm not going to feel" approach. It's an easy way out today. We are confronted with so much violence on TV that we must either not feel or become very angry. Adults watch an average of four hours of TV per day. The average preschooler's viewing time is said to be fifty-plus hours per week. (No community carries "Sesame Street" and "Mister Rogers' Neighborhood" that many hours!) How can people watch the inhuman behavior, killings, and degrading of others without responding? Even comedies are no longer really funny. The name of the game is: Cut other people down, and make them look stupid, so that everybody will laugh.

Newspapers are no better. In order to read the business reports, recipes, or sports sections, one must weed through the murders, fires, rapes, and scandals. It's no wonder that even Christians want to put walls around their feelings. It is no wonder that we are afraid to feel.

One in ten persons is institutionalized at some time in his life for emotional illness. What about the other nine? How many are periodically depressed or need medication habitually for stressful periods of their lives? What about the suppressed, tangled feelings that never emerge explosively and result in institutionalization? Refusing to feel would be refusing God's best for us. When God gives us something—be it hands, ears, emotions, tears, or whatever—He has a good reason for it.

How can we retain our sensitivity with the bad news of the world that bombards us daily? Several things can help. We can minimize the time we spend reading newspapers. It's good to know what is happening in the world, but it is not profitable to spend hours each week, shuffling through unnecessary negative input. Perhaps a weekly news magazine would save time and the temptation to read lots of degrading "news." Another help is to limit TV input. Violence, cut-down comedy, and soap operas will dull your sensitivity. We can't avoid or filter out much of the hurt going on in the world. But we can remember that God neither makes it happen nor wants it to happen. We need not let it monopolize our thinking. Controlling negative input will help us resist the temptation not to feel.

Having grasped the truth that God liked her, Judy made a second important discovery. She had lots of creative potential that had been bottled up and frustrated. She had not been secure enough to find ways to express her creativity. When a person is busy trying to look important, she can't afford failure. And expressing creativity usually demands the risk of failure.

As Judy took her attention off herself, she found she could

sense others' feelings easily. She could detect a neighbor's tiredness, discouragement in a friend, and hurt in a relative. Ideas came easily as to how to encourage and help others. A tiny gift, a shoot from a plant, an invitation to breakfast, a note, an impromptu party—Judy was good at coming up with ideas. Energy that had been burned-out before on impulsive anger and hurt feelings could be rechanneled. The effect was like recharging a battery that had once powered a tiny flashlight and now was sufficient to run a lighthouse. It's much more gratifying to sense that you've helped someone through a difficult time than to feel guilty about a temper tantrum.

An emotional person usually has the potential for creativity. David was a feeling person. As an accomplished harpist, his music soothed Saul. He wrote poetry, expressing his moods and life circumstances. Though centuries have passed since he penned the psalms, and our cultures are vastly different, we can still feel with him as we read. We can see parallels in our life experiences. Common emotions span our canyon of differences, and we feel unified with him. What David wrote expresses our current-day feelings. "Save me, O God; for the waters are come in unto my soul" (Psalm 69:1, KJV*). Doesn't this describe our feelings of depression? What greater words can we use to describe our Lord than the eighth psalm?

To read of David's life from 1 Samuel 16 through 2 Samuel and 1 Kings 2 is to read of extreme highs and extreme lows. At one time he led a dance in the street, expressing his exuberance over a victory. At another time he expressed perhaps his greatest sorrow, over the death of his son, Absalom. "And the king was deeply moved and went up to the chamber over the gate and wept. And thus he said as he walked, 'O my son Absalom, my son, my son Absalom! Would I had died instead of you, O Absalom, my son, my son!'" (2 Samuel 18:33).

David's feelings were strong. They usually motivated him to positive action. David has been described as "a man after God's own heart." Certainly God did not disapprove of David's intensity. During his reign the nation of Israel began its climb to power and greatness that would be climaxed during the reign of his son Solomon. David was a great military man. Of course,

* King James Version.

ultimate glory for his victories belongs to God. God used the creativity He instilled in David to accomplish military strategy.

The economic progress of the growing nation did not result from chaotic good luck. David's creativity resulted in productivity. The planning of the Temple and gathering of materials for its building resulted from David's intense love for God directed into organized action.

David's compassion reached out to bring the crippled Mephibosheth to his table, even though he was the grandson of Saul. Tradition would dictate that Mephibosheth, an heir of David's rival for the throne, be killed.

We often read of David's misdirected lust for Bathsheba and what devastation the resulting sin brought. We should not take this incident lightly; it did result in adultery, murder, the death of David's infant son, and intense grief. But we should also acknowledge that the same intensity in David's feelings usually resulted in good. To wish upon David an unfeeling personality would have avoided the sin but denied the blossoming nation of Israel a creative, dynamic king. Saul would not have experienced compassion at the hand of the one he hated. The surrounding nations would not have seen the power of Jehovah Jireh's right arm working through David's administration. Solomon would not have had the opportunity to learn at the knee of a creative man devoted to God. But the supreme loss would be of that for which God had created David—the friendship and fellowship of a man after His own heart. David, full of vigor, creativity, strong desires, and, above all, love for God, was the man God wanted him to be.

If David was indeed a man after God's own heart, we can catch a glimpse of God's heart through David. We know God is a God of love. But I see His love as being more personal when I see it become hands and feet and mouth, as it works through David to invite Mephibosheth to his table. God's anguish over Jesus' death on the cross becomes more real to me as I see it prefigured in David's mourning over Absalom and his infant son. We can't imagine God's emotions, but we can grasp glimpses of them through the man who was "after His heart." We can see a bit more of the reality of our God when it is fleshed out in David.

We can say with accuracy that our emotions are a part of God in us. Genesis 1:27 tells us that we are made in God's image. We might say we are patterned after Him. Just as our creative Maker delighted in instilling creativity in us, our feeling Maker delighted in making us—in making me a feeling person. Now, *that*, my feeling friend, should make you praise the Lord that you are emotional!

Does acknowledging that our emotions are God-given solve all our problems? Of course not. In fact, we will each face at least one new problem that perhaps we have never faced before. It is this—we're different. Now perhaps that doesn't sound so bad. But in our day, it's acceptable to be like everyone else. Our emotions are always a part of us that differ greatly from one individual to the next. It is not "in" to express those differences. To acknowledge that and put that knowledge into action will mean that we will not be masking or suppressing our differences. This is not so popular in a day when everyone is supposed to be equal, to the extreme of being the same. We're moving toward having no identity other than a social security number and a bedraggled picture on a driver's license. As we express our emotions in creative ways we will discover that we don't fit into any rut. (To which I shout, "Praise the Lord!") But it takes courage.

My daughter came home from school one day and matter-of-factly proclaimed, "This family is weird." As she began to enumerate ways our family is different, I began to wonder if some of our living patterns weren't a little extreme. It's tempting to want to fall into a comfortable rut where you won't stand out. Our objective for our children is not that they be identical to the other twenty-nine little people in their classrooms. Affirming their differences takes courage. Accommodating their emotional differences is more exhausting than accommodating their differences in age and interests.

To be creative in using emotional power is to be unique. It violates the rule of "keeping your cool." We cannot make a formula for any given personality type. We cannot say, "This is what you should do with the hours of your day so that you will be productive and happy." The solution will be different for each individual. The creativity expressed has the potential of being positive in the family, in friendships, in the body of believers, and for each of us individually. But we must accept the challenge of being different.

Are you glad that you feel? Aren't you glad you can cry? Don't be ashamed of those tears. God collects them in a bottle (Psalm 56:8). (For some of us He must have a huge jug!) Aren't you glad you can laugh? Do you ever listen to people laughing? Each person makes such a different sound. Some people chuckle, some roar, some giggle, and some shake all over in silence. With all its variation, laughter is always infectious.

Accepting that our emotions are good and God-given is the beginning of feeling good about our feelings. But let's look at each emotion separately. What's good about anger? Why did God create us with the ability to feel guilt? What good can come from depression? How can these emotions be positive energizers in our lives? Let's look at each emotion in more depth.

3
Anger

Anger is probably the most destructive emotion when mismanaged. It commits murder, destroys property, plots revenge, and changes a sweet mouth to a poison-dipped dagger. It is the seed from which bitterness grows. Depression can originate with unresolved anger, though there may be stages of bitterness in between. Battered children, battered wives, burned-out cities, and destroyed nations are its by-products. With our present arsenals and technology, a destroyed world could be the by-product of anger.

In light of that, it may seem that the best way to handle anger is to suppress it. Isn't this an emotion that should be walled off and denied room in our lives? The pain anger brings might be reduced, but the good that results from anger would also be eliminated.

Jesus, our example, experienced anger, and the result was good. Anger is a great energizer. Anger increases our physical power. Anger is a stimulator. We can choose the option of channeling anger in a positive direction.

First, we must recognize that it is not a sin to be angry. Jesus experienced anger, so we cannot label it as sin. When we say anger is sin we build a false foundation. But when we experience anger we *feel* guilty, so we decide we must suppress our feeling. But a suppressed emotion does not energize us. It reveals itself in a harmful disguise. In the case of suppressed anger, the result is bitterness. Our minds may believe that we've dealt with the problem. We've clenched our teeth and smiled sweetly. We've broken no windows, thrown no hairbrushes, and swallowed the nastyisms we wanted to spit at the customer, our boss, or children.

But our stomachs are in knots, or our blood pressures are rising. Now, is that managing anger?

Anger is not a sin. Ephesians 4:26 says. "BE ANGRY, AND yet DO NOT SIN; do not let the sun go down on your anger." The sin is not anger. The sin lies in what we allow to cause us to be angry and in what we do with that anger. We ask for trouble if we do not deal with anger immediately. The God who created us knows sleep and anger aren't comfortable in the same bed. God intends that sleep should restore our bodies. To lie down with unresolved anger is to deny our bodies that restoration we need for balanced living.

What makes us angry? Too often I am angry for the wrong reasons. Someone has bumped my "I am important" sign. Do you have that problem, too? Our self-esteem is based on something we have, and we get upset when someone takes it away. Perhaps our feelings of self-worth are based on who loves us or likes us. And when that person stops loving us—perhaps that person doesn't even like us anymore—we become angry.

Maybe we're breezing along, not battling anger because there's nothing that angers us. There are no big crises in our lives. We'd better not feel self-righteous. That's when we get angry over spilled milk or a snagged nylon, a misplaced memo or a lost parking spot. That is hardly righteous indignation.

Being angry can become a habit, a way of life. It's as though it feels good to have ruffled feathers. A few outbursts may seem to make you sense a new kind of power. Children cower and acquiesce, clerks hurry to speed up a transaction, mate scrambles to please, co-workers get out of the path. It appears we have discovered a new tool to get our way. We use it. We need not be taught to use anger to our advantage. Just allow it a little room and it blossoms profusely. The tongue becomes sharper. Perhaps there's a sense of pride that we have a temper. "Boy, do I get mad! You'd better watch out!" We let people know, so they'll be ready to give us our way as soon as our faces get red and a snarl twists our lips. Before long, we lose the ability to use anger. It uses us.

To give anger room is to go through life like a Mack truck, rolling over people, squashing their feelings, damaging children's

self-images (permanently, except for the grace of God), sometimes abusing our children. Then we excuse ourselves because we
were mad. The results of allowing the habit of anger to grow are
ugly and destructive. Who can reason with a person who has
refined this habit? Who can match words with her? Verbal
battles become one-sided barrages. The angry person's decibel
level is hard to match. Her senses are dulled, and she has no
concept of the feelings she trucks over. Human beings are her
road bed as she gives her anger room. A few nastyisms become a
verbal arsenal of dehumanizing, crippling bombs that are re-
leased at the slightest, most feeble reason.

We may say she's hurting herself more than anyone else. Not
really. She accumulates unhappiness, but consider the expand-
ing circles of anger. Total the damage of a lifetime, or even ten
years, or five, or only one year of the person who has developed
the habit of anger. Add the discouragement of the sales clerks,
the harassed store managers, and the berated police officer (who
may have a hard time enjoying his job anyway). Add the mate
who drinks a little more, or even deserts her, though his heart is
torn over leaving the children. When there are children, add the
sense of inadequacy they develop because they are told they are
nobodies. Angry parents berate their children, whether the
children are the source of anger or not. Mom can't stand the
sight of them; she can't wait until they leave home. Their
developing minds reach a settled conclusion: "I'm really rotten,
What a zero I surely am."

This kind of misdirected anger is behind much child abuse.
We must add to anger's column the hurt and destruction of a
child's life who lives with that picture of herself. At some point
the child will stand up and say, "I am somebody." Maybe it is
with gun in hand. Maybe it is in abusing children. Maybe it is by
covering identity via bottle or pills. Indeed, the angry person
himself doesn't bear the greatest unhappiness resulting from his
habit. Suffering accumulates in every life that touches him

But where do we go from here? How do we break the habit?
And when may we get angry?

Jesus was being harassed by the Pharisees. They made Him
angry. No, He wasn't sinning. He couldn't. He was experiencing
a God-given emotion. We might say He had a right to be angry.
Look how they criticized Him. They were a step behind Him,

trying to undo everything He did. But Jesus was not angry at the
"inconvenience." He was not angry at their opposition. Jesus
could not be angered at inconveniences and opposition. He
knew He was doing His Father's will. He knew He would finish
the task His Father had given Him. Instead, He was angry and
deeply distressed at their stubborn hearts (Mark 3:5). He was
angry at their attitude. His anger was directed at the misplaced
values of the Pharisees. They were protecting laws, not people.
They were concerned with appearances, not realities. Protecting
their prestigious position at any cost was their goal.

The habit of anger often begins with misplaced values. I am
tempted to value neatness and unscratched furniture above my
developing children. This misplaced value is deceptive because
our children should grow up with pleasant, clean surroundings.
But should we allow things to take precedence over people? Our
twisted value becomes the foundation for unnecessary anger.
When our children run with muddy feet over our newly-scrubbed
floor, we can tell them they are dumb and inconsiderate—that
we slave all day for their benefit, and they return the favor by
acting like a bunch of animals—or we can teach them to be
careful and thoughtful of others' work.

Misplaced values make us angry at revolving doors that don't
revolve, long trains, and "holding patterns" at the airport. We
believe that the supreme objective of the world is to get us where
we're going on time. I haven't been tempted to think this
way—since this morning. I ran out of gas in 94-degree Chicago
heat with a friend and my two preschoolers in tow. My daughter
would be coming from orchestra practice to a locked home in ten
minutes. Empty gas tanks are never convenient.

Managing anger is not an optional convenience. It is a
necessity. Knowing the following facts has helped me.

Fact Number 1: Anger is good if it's in step with God.

Jesus was angry when people misused His Father's house. He
was angry at stubborn, hardened hearts. What makes us angry?
Anger can begin when we feel people haven't treated us as we
deserved. Our twisted value says "I'm important because I'm
somebody, and I want all of you to treat me that way." The fact
is that I'm important because God made me and I'm His.
Reasons for anger change drastically when we realize that

foundational truth. Why be angry at people who put us down? When we realize how special we are to God, little threatens us. As maturing, godly women, we can see the person who puts us down through eyes of compassion. We can pray. "God, reach into her life and reassure her of Your overwhelming love. Remove her need to strike out and hurt."

"So I'm supposed to be angry at what made Jesus angry," you say. "Sometimes I'm angry at the wrong things. Sometimes it's confusing. How can I tell whether I'm angry for the right reasons or just plain old mad?"

Answering these questions will help clarify your motivation:

1. What do I do to resolve my anger before nightfall? Anger feeds on itself negatively. We're to deal with it quickly. Resolve it, or make a plan to resolve it as soon as possible.

2. Have I reacted with insecurity to mistreatment? Concentrate on God's love and how special we are to Him. We need to forgive, even though the offender hasn't asked to be forgiven. I often have to ask forgiveness of my children because I acted before I thought or prayed.

3. Will my plan result in good, or am I out to get even? Anger is the catalyst for much planning. The objective of our planning shows our motivation. Do we want to make someone else feel guilty or miserable? Do we want to redeem our reputations? Or do we want to stop the cycle of evil and replace it with good? Do we want to transform ill-will into kindness?

4. Do I go to sleep in settled conviction that God approves of the action I have taken or plan to take? Friends may tell us we have the right to even the balance, to set the record straight. But whose approval are we seeking? Paul says it this way: "But to me it is a very small thing that I should be examined by you, or by any human court; in fact, I do not even examine myself. I am conscious of nothing against myself, yet I am not by this acquitted; but the one who examines me is the Lord" (1 Corinthians 4:3-4).

Let's suppose you realize that you become angry at the wrong things. Maybe your anger is destructive rather than profitable. Acknowledging that is the beginning of managing anger. Choose to be angry only at what angered Jesus. Then when you do experience anger, it will be energizing rather than immobilizing. You will be able to choose not to be angry based on facts.

Fact Number 2: Anger can be habit-forming.

Anger can feel good. Didn't Jesus sense satisfaction at throwing filth and corruption out of the synagogue? Reacting strongly when we feel deeply satisfies an inner appetite. That can be twisted, however, and we can develop the habit of anger, the habit of reacting strongly over small things, anything, everything.

I experienced this with my daughter's bedroom. For a period of time, it looked like lightning had struck a Goodwill box. I would enter uninvited, grab up armloads of dirty clothes, stuff assorted paraphernalia in the wastebasket, and "verbally encourage" my cowering daughter to change her ways. Soon, it was an upsetting experience even to pass her door. The habit of anger was growing. If her room looked neater, I could still find something out of place.

The best habit to replace this kind of anger is the habit of thankfulness. "In everything give thanks; for this is God's will for you in Christ Jesus" (1 Thessalonians 5:18). This habit helped me manage anger when I looked into my daughter's room. I thanked God for her mind and strong body. I thanked God for what she was learning and that I still have a few more years to train her, I thanked God for my love for her, and for her sense of humor. Before long, that room was looking good to me. The clutter shows she's growing, she's alive, she's involved.

Fact Number 3: Anger fills a void.

An idle mind mulls over seeming or real injustices. First Thessalonians 5:8 says to be self-controlled. First Peter 5:8 says be self-controlled and alert. We choose to think about God's Word and what it says about anger. We choose to review Philippians 4:8 in our minds when our old habit of anger twinges our emotions. We rehearse God's Word on peace. "The steadfast of mind Thou wilt keep in perfect peace, because he trusts in Thee" (Isaiah 26:3). "My peace I give to you . . . let not your heart be troubled"(John 14:27).

Another replacement for anger is work or profitable exercise.

Idleness looks for trouble (1 Timothy 5:13). The industrious person who uses energy in profitable ways is less susceptible to anger. Now, I must qualify that statement. The overworked, driven-to-distraction person will also be anger's easy target. But these two people are different. The former is working toward a goal; the latter is trying to prove a point, usually to herself.

To set goals and work toward them—to work for a living, to care for our children, and to improve our environment—consumes energy that will not be available to anger.

Fact Number 4: Anger is soothed by nature.

Being outdoors helps put our anger in perspective. Walk. Look at trees. Feel the wind. Look for signs of animal life—birds, squirrels, nests, butterflies. Somehow, seeing God's creation is especially effective in cooling anger. The rhythm of waves is therapeutic. Dancing aspen leaves calm us. Our minds have a chance to interact with and balance our emotions. Nature lures our minds to weeds in our gardens, a robin pulling an elastic worm. Anger succumbs to the competition for attention.

If getting outdoors is not a viable option, nurture a few houseplants. Water them; get your fingers in the dirt. Nature can be God's therapy for your anger.

It has happened! Anger has been dispelled. Thank God. Perhaps you cannot thank Him for the event, but thank Him in the circumstances. Thank Him for His love for you. Thank Him for His greatness and power that enable Him to work all things toward good. Search for every possible reason to thank Him. Eventually you will be thanking Him that you are no longer controlled by the habit of anger.

Steps to Take

1. Make a list of what angers you.
2. If God would be angry at the item, put "J" beside it for "justifiable."
3. If anger is self-motivated, put "S" beside it.
4. For each "J" item, make a plan of action to change or affect the item (e.g., write your school board or congressman, communicate with your neighbor—kindly, please).
5. For each "S" item respond with one or more of the

following: Ask, "How can I be thankful for this person or circumstance?" Plan an appropriate response in advance. Write a Bible verse on an index card that speaks to the item. When your anger is triggered by this item, take time to recite this verse. Find a hobby or activity that would divert anger.

The LORD is good to all,
And His mercies are over all His works.
All My works shall give thanks to Thee, O LORD,
And Thy godly ones shall bless Thee.
They shall speak of the glory of Thy kingdom,
And talk of Thy power;
To make known to the sons of men Thy mighty acts,
And the glory of the majesty of Thy kingdom.
Thy kingdom is an everlasting kingdom,
And Thy dominion endures throughout all generations.
The LORD sustains all who fall,
And raises up all who are bowed down.
The eyes of all look to Thee,
And Thou dost give them their food in due time.
Thou dost open Thy hand,
And dost satisfy the desire of every living thing.

Psalm 145:9-16

4

Fear

Praise the Lord for our two-story home! I have not always been able to say that. I remember the first night we slept in our present home (or, I should say, *tried* to sleep). If fatigue dictates sleep, I should have slept soundly from the second my head touched the pillow. The move was endless. As we carried in boxes, more miraculously appeared in the truck. (If you're a family who uses a moving company, you'll understand none of this. Only those of us who keep U-Haul in business really know the agony of it all!) My energetic husband started the day with eighteen holes of golf, and I had put in a regular day of counseling.

Then the fun began! Back and forth, up the stairs, down the stairs, pushing, shoving, groaning. If ever a body deserved the right to collapse, mine did. But there I lay, stiff with fear.

This strange house assumed the proportions of a dark monster creaking at the joints. Eerie light patterns moved in and out of undraped windows. Whatever made us leave our cozy little home on Chester Street, anyway? Two stories below me was a basement doorway with outside steps leading up to ground level. There were bushes around those steps. That laundry room door was so far away I would never hear anyone open it. I broke out in cold perspiration. Fear. The devil was looking for a new foothold in my life.

God had blessed us with more space. Though we were not aware of it at the time, my husband's job was going to require increased traveling. Those were both to be sources of blessing to our whole family. But, as usual, the good arrived accompanied by the option for evil. Satan's intention was to entangle me in a battle with fear. And what a clever place to strike! If I could fear

being alone, I would become bitter about my husband's employment. God's call to him was spiritually stimulating. Bob was
thriving, and so was his work. Bitterness and fear on my part
could be passed along to the children. No wonder the devil chose
this vulnerable spot. Fear is a great immobilizer.

That night of fear was to be repeated. A tiny sense of dread
would sometimes creep through my mind as I drove Bob to the
airport. Sometimes the tentacle of fear would wait until darkness
to entangle me. Fear usually takes a tiny possibility that is valid and distorts it, adds to it, and puffs it up, until the reality
is hidden, and we cannot see beyond the grotesque monster
around us.

During my husband's travels I would visualize that dark back
stairway, listening until my ears ached and watching until my
eyes hurt. And then the furnace would whoosh on! My spirit
went through the ceiling, but my body was frozen to the bed. I
did not resemble one of God's victorious children, or a woman
managing her emotions. I had some lessons to learn. Now I am
thankful that God graciously, patiently began to teach me. Fear
is a smothering, suffocating taskmaster.

God used Scripture memorization in my own life to defeat fear.
Some people may be able to reach for their Bibles when they
need reassurance. In my battle with fear, when I needed
Scripture, I was afraid to move, and my Bible was out of arm's
reach.

In the comfort of daylight, I wrote verses about fear on index
cards and memorized them during the routine of the day. Biking with a toddler, I would pull a card from my pocket and review. "There is no fear in love; but perfect love casts out fear"
(1 John 4:18). I personalized Isaiah 43:1. "But now, thus says the
LORD, your creator, O [Miriam], and He who formed you, O
[Miriam], do not fear, for I have redeemed you; I have called you
by name; you are Mine!" In the darkness, those words became
my strength and the prelude to a good night's sleep.

Remember, we said earlier that emotions are God-given and
good. This is important in managing fear. Fear is a basic
emotion; it is necessary for survival. A newborn infant fears loud
noises and loss of support. If we are driving or walking near
railroad tracks when the train whistles, fear results in action.
Fear keeps us from leaning too far over a bridge. It keeps us from

climbing inside the cages at the zoo. (I imagine the animals are grateful for that!) We run from burning houses. We flee the path of the hurricane. We swim only in familiar waters. Fear is God-given. It is good.

Eric was a student who seldom experienced fear. This void in his emotional makeup got him into lots of trouble. One time he broke both wrists experimenting on his motorcycle. One of his scientific "inventions" blew up his neighbor's lamp post. After he told me of a trick he played with fire, I told him he would never make it to age twenty-five. He laughed. I was serious.

I met his mother in an antique shop a few years after he had graduated. At that time he was in the hospital recovering from another experiment. He had built a glider. In order to increase his speed he had tied it to a friend's car. They were speeding through a forest preserve; the car rounded a bend, bringing a grove of trees between the two vehicles. Eric crashed. A little fear might have prevented that.

Scripture views fear in a positive light. The Greek noun *phobos* is used to describe our feeling toward God. We are to reverentially respect him.

We need not fear His power because it operates within His love. A wholesome respect, mixed with awe, makes us want to please Him. Second Corinthians 7:1 describes this. "Therefore, having these promises, beloved, let us cleanse ourselves from all defilement of flesh and spirit, perfecting holiness in the fear of God." The word used for fear is *phobos*: the healthy fear that causes us to act in a way that will result in our good. In the book of Acts the term is used several times to describe the reaction of Christians to miracles demonstrating God's power. A similar word is *eulaheia*, which means caution leading to reverence. We find this word in Hebrews 12:28: "Therefore, since we receive a kingdom which cannot be shaken, let us show gratitude, by which we may offer to God an acceptable service with reverence and awe."

Another Greek word that is translated "fear" has a different meaning. That is the word *deilia*. This word implies cowardice, which is not given to us by God. "Peace I leave with you; my peace I give you. I do not give to you as the world gives. Do not let your hearts be troubled and do not be afraid" (John 14:27, NIV). God gives us "wise" fear, which gives Him the preeminent

position in our lives. We reverence Him. We live by His Word.
We are led by His Spirit. Our lives are characterized by boldness.
By contrast, the world plants fear in us that results in cowardly
living. We think of the endless possibilities of mishaps and
dangers that might happen—people who might hurt us, acci-
dents that might occur. What is the result of those fears? We are
immobilized, afraid to drive to certain places, afraid to be alone.
We cannot function outside our familiar, carefully-laid routines.

My sister was sleeping in her city apartment. She awoke to
something cold and hard lightly touching her neck. A dark form
hovered over her, and another moved in the shadows behind
him. Disgusted that she owned nothing valuable, the background form said, "Take her." She could no longer suppress the
scream inside her. Her visitors ran, though the shrieks brought
no help. She fled to a neighbor's apartment to call the police.
They arrived to find her apartment door bolted from the inside.
While she had been calling for help her attackers had returned
and bolted the door. There was no question why they had
returned. They wanted her.

Linda has a right to be afraid. But she has chosen to give up
that right in favor of healthy living. She has chosen not to let
her mind relive that event, though she is tempted to many
nights. She chose to be an interior designer in the city. As a single woman she chose to exercise *phobos* and *eulaheia*, not *deilia*.

It disturbs me greatly to hear why women don't do things, why
they are not involved. "I don't like to drive that far from home."
"I'm afraid of city traffic. What if I get off at the wrong exit?" "I
don't like to drive at night." "I get so nervous when I'm in a
crowd." "I don't feel comfortable," and so on. Most of those
responses are *deilia*—cowardice. Remember we said that is not of
God. Those fears immobilize us; they keep us from serving and
ministering. They bar us from new, stimulating experiences.

It is difficult to escape from the web such fears spin. Our minds
focus on ourselves—whether we feel competent, not whether we
have an enabling God. We think about whether we're nervous,
or perspiring, or in control of the present situation. The person
who appears to be in the greatest control of her environment
may be the greatest coward. She may be afraid to function in a
situation where she is not holding all the strings. Can we allow
fear to so limit our lives?

In Scripture we find that when God calls someone to do a job, his world expands. People are called to move beyond their comfort spheres and to trust. Did Paul know all the roads and sea routes he had to travel? Did Jeremiah know the emotional stretching of his lament for his people? Did Mary know the pain of losing her Son to the cross when she said, "Behold the handmaid of the Lord"(Luke 1:38, KJV)? Those special servants of God didn't hold all the strings; they didn't see a yearly calendar neatly rolled out before them with bank balance included. They saw their Lord through eyes of faith, and it was enough.

The web of fear has another immobilizing feature. It weaves more tightly with passing time. Emotions increase and strengthen, rather than change or become flexible. Characteristics are intensified with age. How true of fear! The middle-aged coward will have an infinitesimal world after seventy. How refreshing to meet a seventy-seven-year-old woman traveling in Israel! She takes a few trips each year to expand her mind and broaden her interests. How unlike the usual experience of older people. The sad fact is that once fear has spun its web, the constricting happens automatically with each passing year.

And now you may be saying, "That's fine for you to say. You don't know how it feels. You're one of those people who are naturally brave."

No! Remember, I'm the one frozen in my bed when the furnace goes on!

So how does one begin to manage fear? Second Timothy 1:7 summarizes the answer. "For God has not given us a spirit of timidity, but of power, and love, and discipline."

Steps to Take

1. Recognize that the spirit of fear (*deilia*) is not from God. The victory begins with recognizing the opponent. Our first reaction may be to say, "It's only natural," or, "Anyone would feel the same way." Perhaps so. But, as a Christian, power is available that can manage fear.

2   Accept the spirit of power from God. God delights in seeing our faith linked to His power. Whose enabling are you depending on? If you believe that you'll carry yourself

through by your bootstraps, pushing and groping, then you'd better be afraid. You'll have no traction when the going gets slippery. Our fears naturally increase during times when we see problems without solutions. As individuals we find ourselves increasingly more powerless in the face of bigger government, bigger computers, longer waiting lines, and depersonalized living. So much affects us over which we have no control. Victory over fear is supernatural. But we can have it, as our faith enables us to see the limitless power of God. His power is not some ethereal cloud out before us. It is in our hands, in our feet, in our hearts and minds. Kenneth S. Wuest's *Word Studies in the Greek New Testament* describes it as "force of character." We might say "boldness" or "assertiveness."*

3.   Accept the spirit of love from God. We have already seen that our culture has rejected the fact that God is a loving God. If we internalize skepticism of God's love, our fears will increase. What other foundation for caring is there? Many times I visualize myself standing before the throne of my Lord. When I'm afraid, however, I imagine myself climbing into His lap like a child, feeling His strong arms protecting me. Deuteronomy 33:12 says, "May the beloved of the LORD dwell in security by Him, who shields him all the day, and he dwells between His shoulders." Whatever touches my life at that point is permitted by my loving Lord, and He is great enough to make it result in good in my life.

Faith in God's love frees us from fear. Minirth and Meier, in *Happiness Is a Choice,* suggest that we imagine the worst thing that could possibly happen to us and then consider why that wouldn't be so bad after all.* We cannot experience a hurt that God's comfort cannot make smaller.

You may be saying, "I'll gladly accept the spirit of power and the spirit of love. But how can this affect how I feel when I'm immobilized by fear?" The answer is in the fourth step.

* Kenneth S. Wuest, *Word Studies in the Greek New Testament, for the English Reader* (Grand Rapids: Eerdmans, n.d.).

* Frank B. Minirth and Paul Meier, *Happiness Is a Choice* (Grand Rapids: Baker, 1977), p. 171.

4. Accept the spirit of self-discipline. Before we become
fearful, we must take certain steps. How do I prepare myself
to rest confidently in God's power and love when my
emotions are screaming FEAR? I find verses and promises in
His Word that speak to my fear. I memorize those verses,
putting into practice the principle of Philippians 4:8, filling
my mind with what is good and true and pure and thinking
about those things. Philippians 4:8 is followed by a promise
in verse 9: "And the God of peace shall be with you."

First Peter 5:8 and 1 Thessalonians 5:8 tell us to be
self-controlled and alert. This is practical advice. Do you
fear driving alone at night on unknown roads? Make sure
you have a map, good directions, a full gas tank, and your
doors locked. Now go on singing! Sing songs of praise and
promises that you enjoy. Sing all the verses. Those will help
to keep your mind on God, your source of power, rather
than on your fear. As Christians, we can take certain
precautions. "Be alert" means to use the brains God has
given us. God does not want us to be foolish to prove our
faith. He expects us to be wise. Ultimately, it is our faith
that crowds out fear.

I will lift up my eyes to the mountains;
From whence shall my help come?
My help comes from the LORD,
Who made heaven and earth.
He will not allow your foot to slip;
He who keeps you will not slumber.
Behold, He who keeps Israel
Will neither slumber nor sleep.
The LORD is your keeper;
The LORD is your shade on your right hand.
The sun will not smite you by day,
Nor the moon by night.
The LORD will protect you from all evil;
He will keep your soul.
The LORD will guard your going out and your coming in
From this time forth and forever.

                                        Psalm 121:1-8

5

Empathy

Empathy was the emotion Euodia and Syntyche lacked. "I urge Euodia and I urge Syntyche to live in harmony in the Lord" (Philippians 4:2). Not much is said of their relationship and circumstances. They were loyal workers who "shared [Paul's] struggle in the cause of the gospel"(v. 3). They must have been capable women who loved the Lord in order to work with Paul as they did. Somehow, for some reason, their empathy waned.

The word *empathy* is not used in Scripture; our language does not have a word that equals the Greek. Some phrases used to describe this emotion are: "unity of spirit," "one in thought and feeling," "agree among yourselves," "being of one mind," and "living in harmony." Sounds good, doesn't it? It is easy to see that this is a God-given emotion. Our problem today isn't that empathy has intensified and grown out of control. It has been squashed until there is very little around.

Many women lack a close friend. I listened as a small group of women shared some of their deepest aches. The only one that each one shared was the desire to have someone with whom they could communicate intimately, someone they could be transparent with, someone who could empathize with them. The women were all Christians.

Our mobile society restricts cultivated friendships. The average length of residence in one place is five years. That's just long enough to get a good start. We become afraid of forming close friendships, because we don't want to be hurt by good-byes.

Life-styles of women today do not lend themselves to forming close friendships. Women who work have little time for nurturing relationships outside their families. Women at home taking care of their husbands, carpooling, meeting the needs of little people, and managing their households are genuinely busy. Also, it is not only acceptable to keep distance between neighbors; it is often expected. There's a fear of getting too chummy.

My husband and I entered a crowded elevator rising to a ninty-fifth floor restaurant to celebrate our anniversary. It was filled with residents of the intervening floors. No one spoke or smiled. Although they lived but a few feet apart, these strangers stared at their watches, the elevator door, or invisible specks on their shoes.

Sometimes rural areas appear more friendly. A new farmer or rancher is greeted with a warm "Howdy." Unfortunately, ten years later they are still just "Howdying" each other. Empathy isn't encouraged to grow and mature in this atmosphere.

Empathy takes two. Many women are not aware of this until there has been a void for a while or they experience trauma. Often depression makes us aware of the void. We discover that no one knows we're hurting. In fact, there's no one we've been open enough with that we can call to whisper, "Help." Marylu Terral Jeans describes this in "Perspective":

> He whose house is burning thinks all the world's aglow;
> His neighbor, eating dinner, may never even know.
> And when my heart was lying shattered on the ground,
> I thought the world had ended. . . . you didn't hear a
> sound.*

A woman who is unsure of her worth is usually afraid to form close friendships. Since this woman disapproves of herself, she thinks that if anyone gets to know her, that person will find out she's a nobody. She may have many surface friendships, but is afraid of developing intimate relationships.

How do we nurture empathy? Let's look for the foundational facts in Scripture. "If therefore there is any encouragement in Christ, if there is any consolation of love, if there is any fellowship of the Spirit, if any affection and compassion, make my joy complete by being of the same mind, maintaining the same love, united in spirit, intent on one purpose" (Philippians 2:1-2).

* Used by permission.

This verse gives us the foundation for empathy. It does not say, "If you have several things in common, such as income level, tastes in clothing and home decorating, and educational background, be of the same mind." That's the revised "do it my way" version. That version isn't right, and it doesn't work, either. When our income levels or tastes change we find we have little in common, so we have to form new friendships.

When a local body of believers uses this version, they become ingrown and cliquish. People who don't fit the criteria feel like fifth wheels and have a hard time exercising their gifts to build up the body. Women are especially sensitive when this version is used. However, dear sisters, we often write the version and spell out the criteria ourselves.

The first requisite for empathizing is this: Do we draw our encouragement from Christ? That is the exhortation, comfort, and consolation that we have because we belong to Christ. That is a secure foundation for empathy. It doesn't change, because Christ doesn't change. If our empathy were based on the other person in the relationship, it would fluctuate. But we are to imitate Christ, and He consistently encourages, comforts, and consoles us.

Second, our incentive to empathize grows out of love. The word for love is *agape*. This love goes beyond the tender affection of sister for sister. It is love as shown to us by God. It seeks the welfare of the other person. Empathy is based on the kind of love which never comes naturally. We have to choose to exercise *agape*. The only evidence our friend will have that we have chosen to love her is the action that our *agape* love prompts.

The incentive of love includes in it the concept that a process is involved. Rarely are we flooded with a large dose of *agape* love for a person. A process consists of action, resulting growth, action, resulting growth, action, resulting growth, and so on. We can choose to stop the process and stifle the ability to empathize.

The third basis for empathy is the participation in the Spirit. We might call this *fellowship*. Since a person who doesn't have Christ doesn't have the Holy Spirit, there is a limit to the empathy shown between a Christian woman and a friend who doesn't have Christ.

Have you ever run into an old friend from your high school days? You have empathy as long as you can reminisce about the good old days. If you are a Christian and the other person is not, conversation is really a challenge when you've finished rehashing the past. We are to look for common bonds so we can win them to Christ. But the fellowship is missing. One young woman found several surprises at her ten-year reunion. One third of her classmates had already gone through divorce. One-eighth were there with their boyfriends or girlfriends instead of their spouses. Within a few hours, enough alcohol had been consumed that few could even remember the good old days.

Empathy doesn't exist and grow under all conditions. If we don't have the common bond of the Holy Spirit, empathy is limited to shared experience. We have had Christian friends who have moved states away after we had come to love each other. How delightful it is to get a call or a note that they are coming through town again! Over dinner in our home or coffee at O'Hare Airport we try to catch up in precious minutes. In some ways it is as though they had never moved. The empathy we share in the Spirit bridges the distance, the years, and the gray hair.

The fourth foundation for empathy is affection and sympathy. The Greek word for this refers to the source of tender affections in a person. Those affections originate from within rather than from superficial external circumstances.

What builds the superstructure for empathy? Acceptance. In order to empathize we must accept the other person, just as he is. How we struggle with this! Our culture and our human nature program us to conform, to be alike, to be comfortable when nobody stands out from the crowd. We're threatened by differences in other people. As a result, we ostracize the person who is different.

How hard it is for us to accept differences in each other! How often envy, bitterness, jealousy, and anger originate from our refusals to accept differences in each other. We cannot be "of the same mind" if we don't accept one another. No other woman has the same talents or gifts you have. Even if her gifts and talents are similar, God will not call her to use them in exactly the same way as you do. If He did, one of you would be unnecessary.

Perhaps the division between Euodia and Syntyche came because God called one of them to a different ministry after they'd been working together. Maybe one of them believed God had given her marching orders for the two of them. This isn't a problem for women only. Paul had the same problem in his relationship with John Mark. We sometimes think our vision for the other person is 20/20. Beware if God hasn't revealed the same thing to that person. David said God's Word was a lamp to his feet (Psalm 119:105). God doesn't give one person the lamp and ask the other person to stumble along behind in darkness.

We cannot accept each other if we assign expectations to people. God brought a lovely Christian woman to our neighborhood. I mentally tabulated the facts about her. She had raised four admirable children; she had been a Christian twice as long as I had; she was warm and loving. "Aha!" I thought. "Here is my Titus woman." (A Titus woman is a mature Christian woman who helps to disciple another. See Titus 2:3-5 for the specifics.) After some months of building a relationship, I discovered to my great disappointment that God had different marching orders for my friend. There were needs in our local body that He had gifted her to fulfill. Discipling me didn't fit in. I couldn't get on with the relationship God intended for us until I let go of my expectations for her.

We are now great partners in hosting dinners, showers, and other gatherings. We make a great team at turning out hors d'oeuvres, salad puffs, and tables ladened with desserts. We share dishes, recipes, and tired feet. Together we can accomplish four times what we could otherwise do alone. And we enjoy our friendship in the process.

As we accept people for who they are, we find relationships deepening. There is potential for transparency with a variety of people. Our circle of acquaintances changes to friendships. Obviously, we cannot have intimate, sharing relationships with too many people. Out of those friendships, however, our inner circle develops.

We needn't apologize for having an inner circle. Jesus did. He spoke to hundreds, shared hospitality with dozens, discipled twelve, and had an inner circle of three. His inner circle enjoyed a transparency that He shared with no one else.

Jesus spent more time with those intimate friends than with others. His emotional investment in them was great. The same is true for us. It takes time to build relationships in which we are free to be transparent. First Peter 3:8 says, "To sum up, let all be harmonious, sympathetic, brotherly, kindhearted, and humble in spirit." "Humble in spirit" means courteous, with friendly thoughtfulness. The word *hospitality* is often used in relation to this term.

Mary's husband is a pastor. When he was in seminary, she was warned against forming close friendships in the churches where he would pastor. After this advice, she became afraid to form transparent relationships. Pastor's wives need friends, too—close friends who can feel with them. Time demands on pastors are great. Companionship needs of their wives may be periodically unmet. Sometimes wives are expected to attend so many functions that they feel there is not room in their lives for one more thing. Pastor's wives especially need empathy and friendship. And empathy, friendship, and friendly thoughtfulness take time.

Let's say that you would like to develop a close, transparent friendship. How do you begin? Make a list of several people you would like to get to know better. Ask the Lord to help you to mature as you develop the relationships that would glorify Him. Select one or two for special attention based on the following criteria:

1. Is this woman a Christian? The common bond of the Holy Spirit is essential for this kind of relationship.
2. Do you respect this person, based on what you know?
3. Do you have enough differences to be stimulating to each other?

Take time to get to know this person. Call her and invite her to have breakfast or lunch with you. Initially it may be good to meet in a restaurant where you can concentrate on each other. Become acquainted with her family, and introduce her to yours. If you are both married, don't expect your husbands to establish friendships. Transparent foursomes are rare. Remember that your children may not be fond of each other either. Those are not criteria for your relationship.

Discover how you can practice friendly thoughtfulness. Does she like plants, candy, butterflies? Small, inexpensive gifts can be just as special when you've considered what would be meaningful to her. An occasional card can show her you are thinking of her. Drop by with something from your kitchen when her schedule is full and she doesn't have time to fix special recipes. Keep your visit short!

Your time together should include more than just talking. Do some fun things together. Garden, window-shop, go to garage sales or flower shows. Fly kites with your children. Repot your houseplants together. Rigid routines are not the stuff friendships are made of.

How do you have time for each other? No one has spare time. Here are some ideas. Two friends with eleven children between them found they could seldom get together. They both saved their kitchen cleanup until their children had gone to school on Friday morning. One called the other. With long telephone cords, they washed and wiped, started supper, baked, and scrubbed as they talked. Perhaps your preschooler would nap at your friend's home. My friend and I have occasionally napped all four of our preschoolers while we shared. After an hour or so they are up and playing. Meanwhile, we have shared precious, quiet moments together. Do you have a long drive to make? Invite your friend to go along.

Don't feel you must always have a large section of time. Your friendship will never develop if you wait for the ideal moment or stage in your life.

There are disappointments in friendships. Perhaps you discover that the person you thought would be your closest companion doesn't work out. Enjoy what profit there has been in the relationship. Give your expectation to God. Continue praying that the Lord will help you find a few people with whom you can be transparent.

It's hard to be a good friend. Proverbs gives guidelines for friendships. Study this practical book as you develop relationships. As you come to a verse about friends, write down what you can do to implement that verse. Here are some examples. (I substitute the female gender for the male to make it more practical for me.)

16:28—"A perverse [woman] spreads strife, and a slanderer separates intimate friends."

Application: Even close friendships need guarding. I will listen with ears of love to what is said about my friend.

16:29—"A [woman] of violence entices [her] neighbor, and leads [her] in a way that is not good."

Application: My objective is to bring out the best in my friend—not the worst.

17:9—"[She] who covers a transgression seeks love. But [she] who repeats a matter separates intimate friends."

Application: Forgive and forget her mistakes. Be loyal, and keep confidences.

18:24—"A [woman] of many friends comes to ruin, but there is a friend who sticks closer than a [sister]." (The first word "friend" means "neighbor, passing friend, or acquaintance." The second word "friend" means "one who loves, shares goals.")

Application: Be dependable. Help her achieve her goals instead of being an obstacle.

18:6—"Many will entreat the favor of a generous [woman], and every [woman] is a friend to [her] who gives gifts."

Application: Though I want to be generous with my friend, I will not buy her friendship or expect gifts from her.

22:11—"[She] who loves purity of heart and whose speech is gracious, the king is [her] friend."

Application: Pure motives will encourage gracious conversation.

25:17—"Let your foot rarely be in your neighbor's house, lest [she] become weary of you and hate you."

Application: Don't overstay your welcome. Do not "drop in" when others are there, unless she has specifically invited you. She has other friends and relationships to nurture.

25:20—"Like one who takes off a garment on a cold day, or like vinegar on soda, is [she] who sings songs to a troubled heart."

Application: Share your friend's feelings; don't deny them.

26:18-19—"Like a madman who throws firebrands, arrows and death, so is the [woman] who deceives [her] neighbor, and says, 'Was I not joking?'"

Application: Don't be a practical joker.

27:10—"Do not forsake your own friend or your father's friend, and do not go to your [sister's] house in the day of your calamity; better is a neighbor who is near than a [sister] far away."

Application: Be sensitive to your friend's needs. Stand by her during times of crisis. Support her relatives.

27:14—"[She] who blesses [her] friend with a loud voice early in the morning, it will be reckoned a curse to [her]."

Application: Be thoughtful of characteristics and habits of your friend.

27:17—"Iron sharpens iron, so one [woman] sharpens another."

Application: Discuss differences openly. Sharpen your minds. Disagreements can build a relationship when you communicate well and accept your friend.

Proverbs usually stimulates other ideas for study. Make applications for the verses that refer to the tongue. Include James 3 in this study. I have to keep reminding myself that all my study isn't practical unless I'm applying what I'm learning. Remember, one of our principles is that emotion follows action. As we do the things that a good friend does, as we think what a good friend thinks, we begin to feel empathy.

Steps to Take

1. Determine whether you are developing the emotion of empathy. Answering the following questions may help: Do I have an inner circle of friends with whom I can share my innermost feelings? Are there events and circumstances in

my past that prevent empathy from growing? Am I willing to allow those circumstances to control me, or shall I choose to mature in relationship to this emotion?

2. Select a few individuals with whom you will try to develop a transparent relationship.
3. Reorder time commitments to make time for developing relationships. Be creative! It's a necessity.
4. Study Scripture on friendships. Sometimes the word *neighbor* is used.
5. Apply these instructions as the relationship develops.
6. Give your expectations of the relationship to God.

How blessed is the man who does not walk in the counsel
    of the wicked,
Nor stand in the path of sinners,
Nor sit in the seat of scoffers!
But his delight is in the law of the LORD,
And in His law he meditates day and night.
And he will be like a tree firmly planted by streams of
    water,
Which yields its fruit in its season,
And its leaf does not wither;
And in whatever he does, he prospers.

May those who wait for Thee not be ashamed through me,
    O Lord GOD of hosts;
May those who seek Thee not be dishonored through me,
    O God of Israel.

                                        Psalms 1:1-3; 69:6

6

Envy

Two couples had been friends for a long time. Allen and Pete were college roommates. The girls they married became friends. Through lean years of getting started, they ate pizza together, moved each other via U-Haul, and camped. Year twenty-nine in their lives became the year of change. Pete unexpectedly inherited his uncle's cabinet-making business. It demanded ten hours a day of coordinating workmen, sometimes involving hard labor, and often three night hours of bookwork and planning. But it paid off. Money rolled in. Their second child was born. At age thirty, they moved from their second-floor flat to a home on a wooded acre with access to a lake.

Allen, at age twenty-nine, decided to return to divinity school. Susan packed their "early attic" and secondhand treasures. She scrubbed the kitchen cabinets for their third home—an apartment in married housing near campus. An inner satisfaction of knowing this was what God wanted them to do made up for the exhaustion of moving with an active eighteen-month-old boy.

At mid-quarter test time, Pete and Sally invited them out for pizza after a grueling week of study. Allen and Susan were quiet as they drove up. During greetings and laughter their eyes took in the new pieces of furniture, the kitchen complete with dishwasher, garbage compactor, and microwave. Susan hesitated at the nursery door, taking in the cheerful wallpaper, fuzzy new carpeting, matching furniture, and toys enough to stock a store. She remembered the converted closet where her baby slept, the old dresser drawer where his "wardrobe" lay, leaving room for some blankets, and the third-hand hobby horse in a corner of her kitchen.

As Allen and Susan left, they thanked Pete and Sally for a good time and said that they'd all have to get together again soon. But in the weeks that passed, Susan thought of the mistakes Sally was making raising her two preschoolers. Those were imagined. Envy makes one twist any behavior in the other person from positive to negative. She also imagined that Sally hadn't really treated her like a close friend. They usually got together on her birthday, and Sally hadn't even called her that week.

When Susan was with a group of mutual friends, she made a cutting remark about Pete and Sally. Everyone laughed, because it was clever, so Susan made a few more. Later she felt guilty. She happened across a verse in Proverbs about the tongue and decided she'd better work on her tongue problem.

Susan felt more uncomfortable all the time around Pete and Sally. But she found an easy solution. Allen's busy study schedule allowed them little time or money for socializing, so Susan didn't have to face them often. Her envy destroyed their level of friendship and sharing.

Does Susan's problem seem like a minor one? It isn't. Her friends may never know of her attitude, but Susan will. Like pollution, dumping into a river and rippling outward, her envy will affect Allen first, but others later.

Susan's tongue problem was just a tip on the iceberg of envy. The third chapter of James deals with the tongue: "But if you harbor bitter envy and selfish ambition in your hearts, do not boast about it or deny the truth" (v. 14, NIV). Envy may not be our tongue problem, but if it is, we will never solve our tongue problem until we manage our envy! James tells us not to deny the truth. You can't manage envy until you admit that it's managing you. Susan could bite her tongue and suppress words, but her underlying envy would be untouched. How hard it is to admit that we are envious.

What fact do we need to know to manage envy? We must realize and understand that living in God's will results in good for us as individuals. This truth had been twisted or perhaps lost in the shuffle of Susan's life adjustments. Though Susan would not have whispered it with her mouth, her heart was shouting.

"Lord, I don't approve of how you're providing for me. I don't like the situation You put me in. And, Lord, I don't feel like praising You for the roof over my head, because I'd like a different roof."

It's possible that Susan will live all her life—divinity school to pastor's wife to whatever—looking at the green grass on the other side of the fence. If she does, she'll never see the sunflowers, colored leaves, moss, pinecones, and roses on her own side. Her husband's ministry will suffer, and her children will be denied a joyful mother, but Susan will suffer the most. The riches that God showers on all of His children who praise Him will go unseen and will not be invested in her life.

God could have prevented Susan's battle with envy—and ours, too. He could have made us all alike and given us the same jobs to do. He could have given us identical intellectual capacities, reasoning powers, and physical strengths. We could all have identical personality profiles and preferences. He could have ordained that all homes be identical and that our tastes in food and clothing be identical. Other people's things wouldn't bother us. We would never experience jealousy. We would all be alike. Sounds tremendously boring to me. What do you think?

God ordained differences. God intends for good to result from our diversity. Variety provides for ecological balance in nature. Balance and great satisfaction can result from variety in human beings. Healthy competition results from differences. However, competition becomes deadly to our emotions when our sense of well-being, our sense of worth, depends on being better than anyone else in one area. Dr. James Dobson covers this in his book *Hide and Seek.** This deadly competition breeds envy and jealousy, rather than a positive self-concept.

"Do nothing from selfishness or empty conceit, but with humility of mind let each of you regard one another as more important than himself; do not merely look out for your own personal interests, but also for the interests of others" (Philippians 2:3-4). We are not to value our uniqueness at someone else's expense, and we can seek their honor without putting ourselves down.

---

* James Dobson, *Hide or Seek,* 2d ed. (Old Tappan, N.J.: Revell, 1974).

Sometimes we mistakenly believe that envy is a greater problem today in our nation because of the stress on materialism. I doubt it. We find examples of envy in Scripture that were based on greed for position, beauty, and popularity.

Second Samuel tells us of Jonadab—friend spelled E-N-E-M-Y. Jonadab was a man of few words. He didn't have to say much. Second Samuel 13:3 tells us, "Jonadab was a very shrewd man." Jonadab was Amnon's friend, although the advice he offered ultimately resulted in Amnon's death. They were cousins; Amnon's father, King David, was the brother of Shimesh, Jonadab's father. We are not told how Jonadab won Amnon's friendship. Maybe they roamed the hills around Jerusalem together; maybe they hunted together. They spent enough time together that Jonadab could sense Amnon's moods by looking at him.

"Why the dark circles under the eyes, friend?" Jonadad asked.

"I'm lovesick," was the reply. But that was a lie. Amnon was not in love. He was consumed by lust. The object of his desire was an off-limits woman—Tamar, his half-sister. She was undoubtedly beautiful and in all probability pledged or engaged to someone else. She was not slated to marry Amnon.

Jonadab, as Amnon's friend, could have given him good advice. He could have suggested Amnon ask for Tamar in marriage. He could have protected his cousin Tamar by reminding Amnon that such a relationship would degrade both of them and discredit the leading family of the kingdom. Since Jonadab was shrewd, he probably could have distracted Amnon and helped him concentrate on something else if he'd wanted to. But we sense that Jonadab wasn't looking out for anyone but himself. Maybe he thought the throne could ultimately be his if enough incest, hatred, and revenge ravaged the first family. The account doesn't tell us his motivation. I suspect, however, that envy and jealousy reached their tentacles into his mind.

Jonadab's advice to Amnon was the opposite of Paul's instruction to "make no provision for the flesh in regard to its lusts" (Romans 13:14).

"Go to bed," he advised. "Pretend you're sick, and when your father comes to check on you, tell him you need Tamar's tender-loving care and cooking to bring you back to health."

You can fill in the rest of the story. Amnon's lust was stronger than Tamar's pleas and reasoning. By Jewish law Tamar's calls for help should have sentenced Amnon to death by stoning. But, Amnon had sent the household help away.

There is no such thing as satisfying lust. Fulfilling lust either stimulates the appetite or is revolting. Amnon's lust was not quenched; it merely changed faces and became hatred. Poor Tamar, the beautiful young woman who had entered Amnon's house, left on a path that changed history. Her personal life was like the richly ornamented robe she wore, signifying that she was a virgin daughter of the king. She covered the beauty with ashes, tore the fine pattern, In a small way this would mirror the desolation that moved over her life like a cloud.

Is this the sad ending? Would that it were! James 3:16 tells us ". . . where you have envy and selfish ambition, there you find disorder and every evil practice" (NIV). The king's family was no exception. Tamar's brother, Absalom, quickly discerned the situation, and a triangle of hatred was formed. Absalom's hatred for Amnon had two years to ripen and ferment before his opportunity came to strike. Jonadab's friendly advice had now led to murder. Absalom ordered his men to kill Amnon at a sheep-shearing party when wine had dulled Amnon's senses.

A continuous-motion death pendulum had been set in action. Word spread to David that Absalom had killed all his sons. David had been furious with Amnon's sin but greater grief was yet to follow. When the distorted news reached David, Jonadab was with him, ready to shoot more darts with his mouth. Interestingly, he didn't accompany his "friend" to Absalom's party. Jonadab knew that Absalom was out to get his half-brother, and obviously his friendship was the kind that avoided risks. Jonadab's assurance to David was like rubbing salt in a wound. "My lord the king should not be concerned about the report that all the king's sons are dead. Only Amnon is dead." How did Jonadab know the inside story? Somehow we sense that he was politicking in both parties.

The hurt went on. Absalom ran from the country for three years and, even after he returned, didn't see his father, David, for two years. Alienation had cut ruts into his life which bred revolt. A chain followed with links of deceit, suicide, and dissension. King David left his beloved Jerusalem in flight, fearing his own son. The ugly events that followed brought death to 20,000 men. How can we measure the hurt of broken families, fatherless children, and a nation split with turmoil? The peculiar people, God's example to other nations, were not different. In fact, "disorder and every evil practice" reigned.

And what became of Jonadab? We don't know. We are not told of any high positions to which he attained or any good that he did. His "envy and selfish ambition" do not appear to have brought him much success; instead, he probably had to face consequences in the disrupted kingdom. We may initially think James is an alarmist, overstating the problem of envy. But as we understand how devastating envy is, we must agree.

The root of envy makes a widow look yearningly at a couple eating dinner in a restaurant and think, "Why not her? Why me?" The same root of envy keeps a father from listening with enthusiasm while his friend tells of the touchdown his son scored. Envy keeps parents checking on the scholastic success of their neighbors' children and keeps an employee from wanting his co-worker to do a really good job.

Envy is not the protective feeling we may have for things that are rightfully ours; it is "the feeling of displeasure produced by witnessing or hearing of the advantage or prosperity of others" (*Vine's Expository Dictionary**). This "feeling of displeasure" never dies of natural causes. It is always cancerous. Sometimes it expands a small injury into an ugly, abnormal growth, with external results. When we react with displeasure after hearing about someone else's advantage or prosperity, we are feeling WE should have that advantage, that break, or that bonus. How do we know that what is advantageous for them would be good for us?

Some friends of ours were going to sell their beautiful lakeside home. I began to imagine how wonderful it would be for our children to learn to sail on that lake. How we would enjoy the surrounding woods! I stopped dreaming when my husband told me it was a financial impossibility. I could have felt envy or jealousy toward the new owners. But God had a better option for me. A few months later I began investigating our school system. We knew our children were receiving good teaching, but we dug

---

* W. E. Vine, *Vine's Expository Dictionary of Old & New Testament Words* (Old Tappan, N.J.: Revell, 1981).

a little deeper into the textbooks. I talked with our curriculum director and became acquainted with his philosophy. The facts confirmed that God had us in precisely the place we needed to be. Had we moved, we would have had to find a private school for our children. That district had become entrenched with humanistic philosophies with predictable results. Teaching reading and arithmetic were secondary to teaching "values." Drugs and alcoholism had infiltrated the student body. Praise the Lord that we could not afford to move!

A woman came to me after our neighborhood Bible study one day to tell me of the effect our James study was having on her. Her vocal chords had been removed by surgery and she was learning to communicate again. She discovered that with the great difficulty she experienced now in squeaking out words, she could still fire off "nastyisms" (as she called them). For most of us these result from envy.

Envy does not always become an external, abnormal growth. Sometimes it remains a tiny, internal, poison-producing root. Cutting words are not thrown out. Feeling is submerged, producing at best an uncomfortable "I've got to prove that I'm better" attitude. Or, at worst, "I'm miserable, and the life the Lord gave me is really a bummer." This will eventually have physical effects such as poor health, "nerves," or temporary hypoglycemia. Chronic fatigue and irritability become a way of life.

Where does jealousy fit into the picture? We have said that envy is the feeling of displeasure produced by knowing about the advantage or prosperity of others. Jealousy goes one step further and wants to deny the other person that advantage.

A child sits in his sand castle by the lake, building and patting, pouring water, and imagining. An envious child looks on in gloom. A jealous child destroys the sand castle. Rebuilding the sand castle will bring smiles back to our little construction engineer, but it will not remove the knot in the other child's emotions.

If we could dissect the source of criminal behavior, I wonder what percent would originate with envy resulting in jealousy? We may condemn the criminal, but isn't our own sin just as great when we do not praise the Lord for what He's doing in our lives? There's no room for envy when we look at our circumstances and say, "God, because I believe Romans 8:28, I know You are big enough to bring good from this situation." Deliberately repeating this statement to our Lord, we can follow with praise.

Steps to Take

1. We admit the truth (James 3:14). "Lord, I envy _____."
   We may have to add, "Lord, my envy has turned to jealousy, and I don't want him/her to have _____. I've been secretly wishing _____ would happen to him/her."
2. We accept our differences (Romans 12:3-6). "Lord, help me to use and enjoy the abilities, gifts, physical strengths, and material things you've given me. What I lack is not a problem to You, so I won't let it bother me."

   This exercise may help you: List several things about you for each category:

   My apartment/home is: (example: convenient, cozy)
   My physical strengths are:
   My abilities include:
   My gifts include:
   Lynda Rider, a mother of three and a pastor's wife, lives next door to the church. She completed the exercise like this:

   My apartment/home is: easy to maintain; convenient to my husband's work, church, library, and stores; very low cost to live in.

   My physical strengths are: mind (can learn and think), cooperative hair, clear skin, healthy, strong (can work hard all day), decent weight (can maintain it "fairly" easily).

   My abilities include: talking with people, making friends, encouraging other younger women, speaking, sharing, organizing and decorating a home, and gardening.

   My spiritual gifts include: exhortation.

   Carol Adams, legally blind and a mother of two, had this response:

   My home is: (Contrast) damaged by water (in excess of $56,000.00—even six months later); roomy, with a feeling of room to breathe and move about freely without bumping into things; an older-generation-type of home, expressing my old-fashioned taste/ideas in the interior decorating;

conveniently located, within walking distance of church; the corner grocery store, town, bus, train, and close Christian friends; and private, with a room away from the normal activity of the household.

My physical strengths are: (Contrast:legally blind—less 5 degrees out of 180 degrees sight; hearing impaired—loss of 80% one ear and 50% another) strong will/constitution (do not give up easily and work hard to maintain normal life/functions), sharpened sense of perceiving another person's feelings (because of loss of two senses), can stand ground firmly in something I believe is right, and can do most things very well once shown how.

My abilities include: avid reading, homemaking, and letter-writing.

My spiritual gifts include: encouraging women in small ways (such as a little note, saying, "I'm thinking of you and love you"), a listening ear, praying for others, a willingness to serve where the Lord wants me (He has led me through nursery, child evangelism, Sunday school superintendent, working with women, etc. Guess I like variety-pak!), the ability to dig into God's Word and prepare for sharing.

Both of these women thanked me for asking them to do this exercise. They were encouraged to focus on the positive things in their lives. Lynda was packing for a three-week vacation, and Carol was sitting in her water-damaged home.

3. We declare that God's working in our lives will result in good (Romans 8:28). We may say, "Lord, I can't see how right now, but I'll trust you anyway." Eventually we must search until we find some specific good. "Lord, this loss will force me to depend on You to fill the void. This weakness means I must trust You to fill the gap."

4. We praise God—because He told us to and because we believe differences will result in good.

This attitude manages envy. There is no room for envy after the healing work of praise. Our scars should remind us to begin praising Him as soon as we discern the root of envy trying to gain a foothold.

How lovely are Thy dwelling places,
O LORD of Hosts!
My soul longed and even yearned for the courts of the
    LORD;
My heart and my flesh sing for joy to the living God.
The bird also has found a house,
And the swallow a nest for herself, where she may lay her
    young,
Even Thine altars, O LORD of hosts,
My King and my God.
How blessed are those who dwell in Thy house!
They are ever praising Thee.

Psalm 84:1-4

7

Love

Love is probably the most misrepresented and mismanaged of all emotions. That should not surprise us. The Bible has more to say about love than about any other emotion. It is the greatest motivator. It is to be the primary mark of the Christian. But potential for greatness carries potential for disaster when entrusted to humans. Even Christians can twist love into something unusable at best, but more likely, disastrous. Our culture today illustrates this well.

I heard a song on the radio that went something like this: "Have you got ten minutes? Let's fall in love." As the song progressed, the story line included a married man's propositioning a divorcée. Repeatedly the song twanged, "We'll love all our troubles away." It is highly unlikely that ten years or five years or even *one* year of troubles will be smoothed out by a love affair developed in ten minutes!

With that kind of mental programming through radio, TV, movies, and literature, it is no wonder that love is a confusing emotion. As Christians, we have been influenced by the world's view of love. We have begun to internalize some wrong and devastating ideas. Those ideas are like seeds in our lives—they grow, change our living patterns, and produce fruit.

We are critical of the bad fruit, but we don't identify the seed that produced it. We try to wipe out the symptoms instead of seeking a cure. Unless we identify those seed-causes, they will creep into our thinking, eventually change our behavior, and destroy our distinguishing mark as Christians. God intended for love to be our greatest quality. "But now abide faith, hope, love, these three; but the greatest of these is love" (1 Corinthians 13:13). Does our experience confirm that idea of love? I fear not. Why doesn't it? To find out, we must examine the seeds in our lives.

An old song went something like this: "Once in a while, along the way, love's been good to me." If we were to poll the Christian community, would they rank love as the greatest gift? Would the majority say, "Love's been good to me?"

A dear Christian brother says, "My worst dreams of marriage came true."

A Christian sister told me recently, "I'll never enter a church again."

A child is abused by his Christian parents.

Why the pain? Why the twisted love that hurts? Why the wounds that cannot heal? Why does love mean Hollywood romance and not church relationships? Why is love a word for what happens in parked cars but not for what happens at the family dinner table?

Love is only the greatest when it is lived by the principles of the Person who is love and who created love in the beginning. If we don't allow the originator of a product to teach us how to use it, develop it, and make more of it, the product will likely malfunction.

God is love. Love originated with Him. Without Him, love has one simple result; it will end. We can use the word; we can clang the cymbals; we can splash it on billboards; we can sing of it and dance to its lyrics. But love will be gone. And that's what has happened.

The Bible has been closed. Man and woman—beings who began with dust and will end the same way—have said, "We will write the definition. We will make the rules." And love has gone. In its place warm feelings may linger, but they will eventually grow cold. In its place may be marriage licenses, but they will be dissolved by the courts. In its place a "love child" may be born, but that child will be branded *illegitimate*. In its place church steeples may be built, with bells pealing and light beaming through stained glass windows, but bickering, gossip, envy, and debt will remain within.

How can we have love? How can we manage the emotional side of love? Love can be learned only with the Bible open. Love can enter only a heart that is teachable. Love can make its home only in the person who says, "Yes, Lord, I'll do it Your way." To manage love one must begin by accepting God's foundational truths and eliminating the world's values.

Seed number 1 from our culture says we *fall* in love. There is no truth in Scripture to support this concept. The first marriage was not an accident that resulted from falling. Marriages in the Bible were planned, and mate-matching was a responsible, careful process. Today many marriages are based on emotional attraction. That emotional attraction has been called love, but it shouldn't be. If the emotional attraction is based on physical or common interests alone, then what happens when those are gone? Won't "love" disappear also?

Seed number 2 says that falling in love is beyond our control. Falls are usually unintentional. Since falling in love often results in marriage, that means we have no control over who our life-mates will be! Apparently, they are selected by accident. That sounds ridiculous, and it is. We wouldn't think of investing our money on the basis of feelings. Yet we allow an important relationship—and a key one for the resulting children—to be determined by a "fall."

What is the solution? We must teach our children that they will *select* their lifetime mates. First, a husband or wife must be a Christian. The Bible says so. Next, his character is more important than his pocketbook or any other feature. Examine his parents. No, the couple will not live with them. But most of the parents' values and characteristics are combined in their children, although they, as in-laws, may be miles away.

When we find characteristics we have in common with other people, we can enjoy the things we have in common, but that does not mean we are really in love. If you enjoy eating seafood with a particular friend or discussing politics or watching athletic events together, fine. But that does not mean you should be bed partners or lifetime mates.

Seed number 3 is that love is only a feeling. It is not. It is a complex combination of our minds, our wills, and our emotions. Intense as our feelings may be, they are only the rim of the wheel, not the hub. If we were to examine only the emotional side of love, we would find it extremely complex. A woman may feel attraction for someone because he resembles her father. She will simultaneously attach negative feelings toward him that she felt toward her father, though there is no basis for them. To oversimplify love promotes the popular "take it or leave it" philosophy. Something has to click every moment we're together or we are no longer in love. Anyone who has lived just a little has learned that simply is not true.

Love often requires that we act contrary to our feelings. When our third child was on the way, I received doctor's orders not to lift anything or push heavy objects. Our other children were four and eighteen months old. For seven months my husband pushed the vacuum and lifted dripping children from the bathtub. Do you think he felt like it after a long day's work and hassling his way home in rush-hour traffic? His reward was another squirming boy who would cost him $25,000 to raise and untold hours of talking, wrestling, and pitching balls. If Bob's love had been based on feeling, it would have been drained faster than his pocketbook.

Seed number 4 says that love is temporary. But God says it is permanent. He sets the example in John 3:16. He loved the world, always—before obedience and after. Jesus fleshed out that love. Our marriages are to be examples of His permanent love.

In His love, God shows the truths that uproot seed number 5. This seed says that there are no ground rules. You can inflict any kind of devastation and make it disappear by saying, "I love you." Our culture glibly says, "All's fair in love and war—and sometimes you can't tell the difference." That's a telling comment on our sick society.

Love—as God defined and demonstrated it—refuses to be an isolated gift wrapped around any kind of behavior. When we throw out the patterns of behavior, the attitudes, and His definition, love isn't there. Eventually we discover that what we thought was love was only a facade, and disappointment creeps in with hurt and pain. The facade crumbles. First Corinthians 13 gives us some behavioral guidelines for love. We may not measure up to all of them all of the time or even all of them some of the time. But we'd better measure up to some of them some of the time, or we're not loving.

I have a friend whose husband says he loves her. He never supports her, looks out for her interests, or emotionally encourages her. He has never got to know her as a person, yet he expects such from her. That's not fair. It's not love, either.

Seed number 6 says that love is an isolated element of our lives. The biblical fact is that love permeates our whole beings, affecting every part of our relationships. To many people, love is concerned only with the physical relationship. But God's guideline is the opposite: love is not part of sex anytime except in marriage.

We plan to love. We expect permanence. We know love will demand. And we realize love will permeate every part of our being. It will affect our working relationship if intimacy with a co-worker violates God's principles. It will affect our children and their attitude toward their fathers if we criticize our husbands. It will affect our sons' masculine identity if we leave our husbands. Love is not an isolated emotion. What we do in the name of love will affect our total beings. Our jobs will be affected, our marriages, our children, our friendships. Each person who is touched by our lives will be affected, be it child or grocery check-out person.

Our children vote as we do, talk as we do, become educated to the extent we are, wink or make hand gestures as we do, play as we do, and drink as we do. Their attitudes are shaped by ours. They learn to love by mimicking us. They hate what we hate. Deuteronomy 5:9 tells us that children suffer to the third and fourth generations because of the sins of their fathers. This is not a harsh and unloving God saying, "You sinned. I'll punish your grandchildren for this." It is a God of consistent principles who knows the mistakes made by parents chart a course that the children follow. They naturally imitate their parents and suffer the same consequences, though they may have vowed to be different.

I have a friend who is a member of Alcoholics Anonymous. Her father was an alcoholic. She vowed she would not wreck her mate, destroy her marriage, and beat her children as he did. But by age fifteen she was on the bottle. Later she abused her children. Her marriage was a disaster. She followed the course her father had marked out for her. Except for God's intervention, this pattern would have been repeated generation after generation.

My friend decided to accept God's love through Jesus. This opened the floodgates for God to teach her love by His dimensions. As a single parent with three children to raise—and enough insecurities and bad habits to wreck all of their lives—my friend began a new adventure. Her pressures multiplied. She was out of money with a family to support, out of patience with three small children clinging to her like parasites, and out of love with three beings programmed to imitate her. God took over. "If you have died with Christ to the elementary principles of the world, why, as if you were living in the world, do you submit yourself to decrees?" (Colossians 2:20).

My friend rejected this world's basic principles. Instead, she learned a new way to love. The course of her life has changed. Her children now have a secure mother. She may remain in Alcoholics Anonymous all of her life. But her children will not suffer the abuses she did. I watched her four-year-old son rough-housing with his friends. How beautiful it was to see a normal boy—secure, active, aggressive, able to make friends, and willing to trust. The chain of sin has been broken by love.

Seed number 7 says that love exists for the present. Listen to current love songs. They are full of phrases like "Let's forget all about tomorrow." One even says "Let's do something we'll regret tomorrow." God's guidelines never neglect the future. We mismanage our emotions when we live any way we please. Then when we are lonely, insecure, and loaded down with guilt feelings we say, "Love is the greatest. I'll find someone to love me, and everything will be OK."

But it isn't. So we try to find substitute loves. But that doesn't fill the void; our insecurity is still there. We find a new bed partner. Or we divorce to find someone who we hope will accept us for who we are. But the frustrations simply multiply, and we say, "Love isn't the greatest, after all." Actually, love was never there in the first place. The selfish life-style has no room for love; love cannot exist in the tangle of emotions that rejects God's truths. "See to it that no one takes you captive through philosophy and empty deception, according to the tradition of men, according to the elementary principles of the world, rather than according to Christ" (Colossians 2:8).

First Peter 4:8 tells us that love covers a multitude of sins. In order for love to cover our sins, Jesus, God's only precious and much-loved Son, had to die. God's unconditional love is available only after we've met His condition: the acceptance of His Son. If a person has not accepted Jesus, God's Son, love cannot cover his tangled emotions and rebuild his wrecked life.

God's love is demanding. It required that He turn His back on His only Son. Jesus' love for His Father is demanding. It required that He lay aside His feelings and His desires, and say, "Not My will but Thine be done" (Luke 22:42; cf. Matthew 26:39, 42, 44; Mark 14:36). Love does demand—not its own way, but God's.

There is no love without sacrifice. And sacrifice looks to the future at the expense of the present. A husband sacrifices to provide for his family. He feels like sinking into the easy chair with newspaper and earplugs in place. Instead, he romps with the children and fixes a clogged drain. A mother aches for a full night's sleep, but her infant rouses her, needing to be nursed. A frightened child needs to be rocked and soothed. Our mate is experiencing stress; fatigue has wiped the smile from her face or the ruddy color from his cheek. We sacrifice. We expend energy to take up the slack and lighten the load. We spend minutes fixing his favorite spiced tea, and cheering him when we're weary ourselves. Yes, love demands. Love requires our feet, our hands, and our emotions to respond to its demands. The emotion that will not sacrifice is not love.

God's definition of love looks beyond today to the future. As the Father turned His back on His only Son on the cross, surely He saw the resurrection. As Jesus said, "Not My will," surely He saw the day when He would stand before His Father with all of us—His trophies.

Love looks to the future. Love says, "Look into the future. Do you see your children as they would develop with only one parent—one parent who likely must work, care for a home, and in leftover minutes, love these children?"God's love says, "Live by My principles of permanence, and I will take care of the future. Live by My principle of fitting in with each other's plans, and I'll take care of the feelings. Love by My principle of commitment, and I will cover the multitude of differences." Love looks to tomorrow. Love intends to be present tomorrow. It doesn't stand with one hand on the door to make a hasty retreat when the going gets rough.

Love is planned. That's part of God's definition. Before we

were born—in fact, before the earth was formed—God, Jesus, and the Holy Spirit planned how we would have access to Their family. They determined They would love us before we were even conceived. There was no falling or stumbling into love and all it demanded. Our definition of love should be the same. Love is planned. Young women must plan to love their husbands. There is no room for a wait-and-see attitude. "Maybe he'll meet all my expectations." (No man is that perfect; besides, if he were, marriage would ruin him.)

A couple plans to love their child. "If this child is cute and bright, we'll love him." (Beware! The brighter a child is, the more trouble he will get into, and at an earlier age. Sometimes clever children are harder to love!)

A Christian plans to love other Christians. "If this Christian is like me, we'll form a close, warm relationship." If the Christian is exactly like you, one of you is unnecessary, and you'll get on each other's nerves because you understand each other too well.

Seed number 8 tells us that love is the same thing as instant intimacy. A recent newspaper article described the search of our youth for instant intimacy. Dr. Luella Klein, officer of the American College of Obstetricians and Gynecologists, said that peer pressure is increasing among single teenage girls to have a baby and keep the child. Girls want to prove that they are feminine and that they have a boyfriend. They are searching for instant intimacy. They hope their babies will help to satisfy this desire.

The desire for intimacy and deep knowing of another person is not accomplished by superficial friendships or even pregnancy. Unfortunately, young girls discover that after another life has been born into a setting that is not what God intended. The young girls' life patterns are not set, and they usually do not complete school; their lifetime potential is often thwarted. They tend to strike out on their own because they don't want to be with their families. But they cannot cope on their own. Dr. Klein says these young mothers are frequently child abusers. Thus, instant intimacy is a fantasy that does not result in love for the young girl or her child.

God's foundational truth regarding love is this: It must be done His way. What a simple truth, but how we struggle to reject it. There will be no sure foundation for love until we can say, "Yes, Lord, Your dimension of love shall be mine. I shall meet the demand of Your love in order to have it." We step forward. We say with confidence, "Yes, Lord, my love will be planned by Your standards; my feelings will follow." We learn love, sometimes walking, sometimes running, as we think of the other person and of the future.

Sometimes we cry, "Lord! It isn't fair!"

"I know, child," He answers. "But it will be someday. And I will out-love any hurt you experience when you love by My definition."

And that is a promise no one else can make.

Love takes on God's dimension. It is not a roller-coaster emotion that keeps us spinning, but a totally enveloping state of living—comfortable and at the same time intoxicating; soothing yet exciting; exhausting but energizing; draining but filling to overflowing; our greatest sacrifice, yet our greatest reward. "The greatest of these is love."

Steps to Take

1. Planning for permanence in a relationship gives us the incentive to adapt to each other. Think of a relationship in which you'd like to grow (e.g. mother-in-law, friend, husband or wife, child). What adaptations could you make that would help love grow?
2. List several characteristics about that person that you admire.
3. Communicate those to the person. One woman printed a sign that said, "I love you." One day she stood on a corner that her husband's bus passed, holding her sign. Her husband couldn't wait to get home. (If your husband would be embarassed by this, please do not do it.) Take your mother-in-law out to lunch on your husband's birthday. It was a big day for her, you know. Take your child out to a place she wants to eat and tell her what you admire in her. Give your friend or child a blank time check. It can be filled in with something they want you to do with them or for them.

For you have made the LORD my refuge,
Even the Most High, your dwelling place.
No evil will befall you,
Nor will any plague come near your tent.
For He will give His angels charge concerning you,
To guard you in all your ways.
They will bear you up in their hands,
Lest you strike your foot against a stone.
You will tread upon the lion and cobra,
The young lion and the serpent you will trample down.
Because he has loved Me, therefore I will deliver him;
I will set him securely on high, because he has known
    My name.
He will call upon Me, and I will answer him;
I will be with him in trouble;
I will rescue him, and honor him.
With a long life I will satisfy him,
And let him behold My salvation.

Psalm 91:9-16

8

Anxiety (Worry)

The octopus of our emotions has a tentacle called worry. We usually underestimate its strength and allow it to do the damage it does, because we know if we just can't tolerate it anymore, there's plenty of medicine on the market to neutralize it for a while. If we worry until that dull, throbbing headache sets in, we can just take a couple of aspirin. That's acceptable in Christian circles. Aspirin-taking is not a sin. If worry wraps us even more tightly, we have another alternative: sleeping pills. Anxiety tends to produce insomnia, but a trip to the drugstore can solve that. (Hopefully, you aren't in your long johns and nightcap, with your eyelashes and perhaps your teeth on the bathroom counter when worry sets in and you need that sleeping pill.)

As Christians we know we're not supposed to worry. So we don't call it "worry." We just say we're "burdened" or "concerned."

We're "concerned" over our relationship with our in-laws. Will all the money we're paying into Social Security be available to support us when we're sixty-five? Will inflation rob us of a pleasant retirement? Will the companies we work for remain sound and able to meet payroll? Will our children turn out all right? Will our old roof last until we can afford another? Is that strange ache in our sides cancer or old age?

On and on goes our list of concerns. I once read that the sexual promiscuity of recent years was set off by the use of the H-bomb in World War II. Young people were worried that their lives would be shortened, so they tried to pack all the living they could into their youthful years.

We can use "concern" to justify all kinds of hurtful and wrong

75

behavior. Anxiety over losing a relationship can result in premarital or untimely pregnancy. Anxiety over living a life of aloneness can lead to a mismatched marriage. We say we can live with worry, and the medicine on the market will help us. Is this true? The price of worry is too great.

King Saul offered the sacrifices that only the priest Samuel was supposed to offer. Why? Because he was worried that Samuel wouldn't make it to the occasion on time (see 1 Samuel 13:8-14). Later he visited a witch to attempt a seance with the deceased Samuel because he was worried. He was confused, and he didn't know what to do. He no longer put God first, so he was out looking for quick answers (see 1 Samuel 28:3-19). Saul's worry led to disobedience and then the loss of his kingship. The worst result was his separation from God.

How many times has our worry caused us to jump in hastily and act when God had a different time schedule? Abraham and Hagar begat Ishmael because of Sarah's "concern" over God's timing in providing children. Abraham and Sarah's worry and subsequent disobedience has resulted in bloodshed throughout centuries. The price of worry is too great.

Webster defines anxiety in this way: "painful uneasiness of mind over an impending or anticipated ill; disquietude over a possible or impending ill or unknown future event."

King Saul was disquieted over his people's fear when the Philistines were gathering for war. Later we find him disquieted over the fact that he couldn't talk to Samuel or communicate with God.

Sarah was disquieted over the lack of an heir.

Martha was disquieted over whether a meal would be served properly and on time (Luke 10:38-42).

It's easy to find a reason to be disquieted. If we empty our minds, worry is the first to find the empty space. Like a rabbit, worry is a prolific reproducer, and its offspring require room. What spiritual price do we pay for worry? We find the answer in the parable of the sower.

Hear then the parable of the sower. When anyone hears the word of the kingdom, and does not understand it, the evil one comes and snatches away what has been sown in his heart. This is the one on whom seed was sown beside the road. And the one on whom seed was sown on the rocky places, this is the man who hears the word, and immediately receives it with joy; yet he has no firm root in himself, but is only temporary, and when affliction or persecution arises because of the word, immediately he falls away. And the one on whom seed was sown among the thorns, this is the man who hears the word, and the worry of the world, and the deceitfulness of riches choke the word, and it becomes unfruitful. And the one on whom seed was sown on the good soil, this is the man who hears the word and understands it; who indeed bears fruit, and brings forth, some a hundredfold, some sixty, and some thirty. [Matthew 13:18-23]

The last two kinds of people mentioned in this story were both Christians; they both accepted God's Word, and it took root in their lives. But one was a productive Christian, and one was not. In the case of Mary and Martha, being God's woman made a visible difference in one person and not the other. Don't we see this today? Some Christians never seem to mature from caterpillars into God's butterflies. What makes the difference? In many cases, worry.

Luke describes it this way:

The seed that fell among thorns stands for those who hear, but as they go on their way they are choked by life's worries, riches and pleasures, and they do not mature. But the seed on good soil stands for those with a noble and good heart, who hear the word, retain it, and by persevering produce a crop. [Luke 8:14-15, NIV]

If the devil can be successful in filling our minds with worry, he can rob the Lord of productive Christians. Others will observe the worrying Christian's life and say, "No, thanks. Who wants what they have?" Worrying cannot rob us of ultimate salvation, but it ravages the present and stalks the future. The potential for "manifold more in this life" is squashed.

I talked to a Christian one day who was nearing death. Filled with anticipation for him, I asked, "Aren't you excited about seeing Jesus?" How sad I was to hear his answer. He couldn't leave this earth yet. His wife needed him. Work needed tending. "Can't you see, Miriam? I can't look forward to those heavenly things." The cares of the world were choking him. The joy of a fruitful harvest had been smothered. There was no radiance or excitement in his tired, gray eyes.

Why do we insist on worrying? This issue is bigger than aspirin and sleeping pills, fidgeting and making decisions ahead of or behind schedule. The bottom line is this: We don't really believe God will meet our needs. If we did, we would not worry. Who is in charge of meeting our needs? And who determines what is a "need" or a "want"?

Consider these promises. "Be anxious for nothing, but in everything by prayer and supplication with thanksgiving let your requests be made known to God. And the peace of God, which surpasses all comprehension, shall guard your hearts and your minds in Christ Jesus" (Philippians 4:6-7). "And my God shall supply all your needs according to His riches in glory in Christ Jesus" (Philippians 4:19).

> And He said to his disciples, "For this reason I say to you, 'do not be anxious for your life, as to what you shall eat; nor for your body, as to what you shall put on. For life is more than food, and the body than clothing. Consider the ravens, for they neither sow nor reap; and they have no storeroom nor barn; and yet God feeds them; how much more valuable you are than the birds!'" [Luke 12:22-26]

It sounds as though people in Jesus' time were worrying about the things we worry about today: security for the future, unpaid bills, grocery budgets, wardrobes, dying, whether we'll do everything we've planned to do, inflation, our health, how we feel. Yet Jesus told them not to worry about such things. We've heard the teachings, but there's a step further: Are we retaining those facts and acting on them?"

Why should we worry when our God has committed Himself to satisfying all our needs? I suspect we're afraid He'll classify some of our "needs" as "wants" and not supply them. "But, Lord," we plead, "You said you wanted to give me the desires of my heart." Watch out anytime you find yourself praying, "But,

Lord." You're probably trying to argue with God. Why argue with One who is more committed to your success than you are?

"Yes, Miriam," my Lord answers. "But remember what I told you before I promised to give you the desires of your heart? You are to delight in Me above all else [see Psalm 37:5]. Have you met My condition?" Hungering for more of my Lord will crowd out many of my wants. "But seek for His kingdom, and these things shall be added to you" (Luke 12:31).

Let's take a closer look at what our needs are. Minirth and Meier in *Happiness Is a Choice* list these twelve needs:

1. air
2. food
3. water
4. stimulation
5. sex
6. love
7. self-worth
8. power
9. aggression
10. comfort
11. security
12. relief from psychic tension (p. 75).

God does not intend to deny any of our needs. As we read His Word (e.g., Romans 12:9-21), we learn living patterns. We absorb behavioral patterns that have the greatest potential for meeting our needs. God's world has the potential for providing air, food, and water to every individual in it. His institution, the church, provides the source for meeting many of those needs. Interacting with other people stimulates us. Another of his institutions, the family, has the potential for satisfying needs for love, comfort, and security. Marriage provides the potential for satisfying sexual needs. Caring for the earth, making it productive and beautiful, satisfies our need for power, self-worth, and aggression. And living by God's loving guidelines frees us from psychic tension. God lays before us the potential for supplying each need.

How do our lives get twisted so that our needs go unmet? We

defy God's instruction for living. Puny men and women turn their backs on God and tell Him they will manage the earth in their own way. What results? Food is wasted on one side of the planet, while people starve on the other side. People live in families, work in offices surrounded by people, crowd into commuter trains, and feel lonely twenty-four hours a day. Marriages exist in which there has been no intimacy for years. Individuals satisfy their aggression by violence and vandalism. National and international political forces struggle for power— not to gain the right to serve the people, but to be able to play "king-on-the-mountain." Politicians grab for all they can while they are on top.

People choose not to read the Bible, God's blueprint for behavioral patterns. Yet when things are topsy-turvy, and people are crying and fighting and hurting—at that point man chooses to look into the heavens and shout, "If there's a God up there, do something. Now that we've ruined the universe, heal it to prove Your existence. Show that You care—our way, not Yours."

We have a need beyond those on Minirth's and Meier's survival list. Our main purpose here on earth is to glorify God, to elevate Him, to spotlight Him. Sometimes that is accomplished through death. God's existence has been broadcast through the persecution of missionaries and other Christians in foreign lands. What happened to their need to survive? If they could speak to us now, I believe they would say that God met all of their needs.

Few of us have had the "right" to worry as Nada had. Her husband had been missing for two days. What do you tell your ten-year-old son in such a case? Her two teenagers kept their usual pace, covering their inner turmoil. Nada knew there had been a crisis at work. Ken's twisted face the last time she saw him wasn't characteristic of her husband. The company men wouldn't talk to her. They said, "Ask your husband." But he was gone.

She was drawn to an old garage where Ken and their sixteen-year-old son had been working on an old car. Ken was there. Carbon monoxide had erased the distortion and life as well. Here is what Nada had written that morning before she found him.

"I give to You, oh Lord, my God, the whereabouts of Kenneth

L. Erickson this day, July 14, and I in faith leave him under Your care, knowing that all is well with his soul! Thank you, Lord Jesus, for your comfort this day and for the joy I and the rest of my family can experience, knowing You are in complete charge."

Nada struggles as a single parent. Needs that were met in her marriage clutch at her like hungry beggars, especially at night. She enters a grocery store where she and Ken used to shop. "Let's get what we have to and get out of here," she says to her son. Nada and a girlfriend go out for lunch on their break. Men from Ken's company sit at a table nearby. They stare at her. "Do I look that strange?" she whispers to her friend. But through it all, Nada tells me that God is meeting her needs. God looks pretty big to me through Nada's life.

If we have to show God our survival list of needs so He can use it as a handy checklist, He really isn't God; He is a dispense-all programmed by us for us. Concentrating on our need list is a good way to miss God as God. The really rich people I know have been through crises that have stripped them. But they later talk about God with real words and honest feelings. Their lives lack clutter. For them, basics like faith and trust are not elusive and ethereal.

God's most exciting gifts for me have been beyond my mundane list of needs. For me, there's usually lots of psychic tension on the path to the treasure. If I could see a sign marked Psychic Tension Ahead, I would take another route. But God wisely balances my struggles of growth with glimpses of new goals and satisfaction.

We shake our heads at the non-Christian who is making demands of God. How can he demand that God show His existence and love by using man's formula? But don't we as Christians do the same thing? "You love me, don't You, Lord? Well, I know my need. Here's how You can satisfy it so that I can praise You. What's that, Lord? That isn't my need? Your answer is 'No?' Your answer is 'Wait'?" The worry buzzer sounds, and we begin to fret. We're burdened. We're concerned.

Yet there is valid concern, which is not worry. How do we know if we have a valid concern or burden, with which God intends to stimulate us to action? How do we separate concern for those issues from worry about things that will distract us from productivity as Christians? Perhaps answering these questions will help us to differentiate between the two.

The Greek word for "care" is defined: "to draw in different directions, distract, to be anxious about, distracting care" (*Vine's Expository Dictionary*).

1. Is my concern causing me to serve God better, with more fervor? Am I glorifying Him in the process? Or is my concern interfering with my service to God? An unmarried person can be distracted by his or her unmet physical need. Or she can be freed to serve God better by being unmarried (1 Corinthians 7:32-35).

2. Is the concern drawing me to communicate with God more often and more openly? Or do I sense a barrier when I pray? Am I distracted in prayer by my thoughts' continually going to the circumstances that confront me rather than to the Lord?

3. Where am I looking for answers? Am I manipulating circumstances in order to achieve what I see as the desired result? Am I putting my trust and hope in people? Do I feel that I must convince those people to come around to my way of thinking?

4. Am I experiencing an underlying calm during this time, or are my emotions totally "up for grabs"?

5. What do I expect to be the result? Am I just hoping to survive, or am I confidently expecting to come out shining like refined gold?

What about your concern? Is it distracting you from being a vibrant Christian? Then you are worrying. As Christians we have the option when life is tough to plaster on a smile and superficially (through clenched teeth perhaps) affirm that we're resting in the Lord. We can go home and swallow a few pills or conceive an ulcer. Or we can get hold of the underlying issue. We can search the Scriptures and live our lives by God's blueprint. We can allow daily Bible reading to filter through our minds and hearts out to our fingertips and the soles of our feet. Then when the tough times come (and you can be sure that they will), the foundation will be there. We will have the assurance of

God's promise that the issues are not greater than He is. His commitment to us is personal, continual, and inexhaustible. In the crucible of hard times we will say with David, "When I said, 'My foot is slipping,' your love, O LORD, supported me. When anxiety was great with me, your consolation brought joy to my soul"(Psalm 94:18, NIV).

Steps to Take

1. Determine whether your anxiety stems from an unmet need or a want. If it is a want, recognize that you might not get what you want. If it seems to be a need, trust God to supply it.
2. God never intends for us to violate His Word to "solve" a problem. If the only available action violates His absolutes, do nothing.
3. Pray about your anxiety. Ask God for peace as well as direction for action.
4. Keep reading the Word regularly. Often you just "happen" to be reading Scripture that speaks to your anxiety.
5. Anxiety is the stuff from which the Lord builds faith. When we're out on risk's edge we often feel uncomfortable. But risk's edge is also where faith grows. Peter never would have felt anxiety if he hadn't stepped out of the boat (see Matthew 14:25-31). But then he never would have walked on water, either!

> The LORD reigns,
> He is clothed with majesty;
> The LORD has clothed and girded Himself with
>   strength;
> Indeed, the world is firmly established, it will not
>   be moved.
> Thy throne is established from of old;
> Thou art from everlasting.
> The floods have lifted up, O LORD,
> The floods have lifted up their voice;
> The floods lift up their pounding waves.
> More than the sounds of many waters,

Than the mighty breakers of the sea,
The LORD on high is mighty.
Thy testimonies are fully confirmed;
Holiness befits Thy house,
O LORD, forevermore.

Psalm 93

9

Discouragement

Failure. The hot tears streamed down my cheeks. Hours of labor wasted. An uphill battle gained inch by tedious inch for a grand prize of nothing. "Lord, do You know what You have done? I was sure I had my marching orders straight from You. How could You have made me do it all for nothing?" I wish I could say I "reasoned" with God. But I wasn't reasoning; I was arguing. How could I have misread Him so completely? The wasted effort had been expensive, not only to me personally, but to my children and my tolerant husband.

"Lord, I've been faithful. See my past record. Look at the hard things you've required of me—the cold nights I was scheduled to speak when my body ached for a hot shower, a book, and a cup of tea; the lessons taught and speeches given with a knotted stomach and knocking knees; the vulnerability of opening my mouth. Wasn't it worth anything to You, Lord?"

The greatest hurt was that it seemed I had misread God's blueprint. How could I have opened my Bible each day, read, prayed, and received peace regarding what I was doing, if it was wrong?

I was arguing with God over a rejected manuscript. That was the tip of the iceberg, anyway. Actually, I had a bigger problem; I was discouraged. I was looking for approval from people, and it wasn't coming. I was trying to earn position with God, and I couldn't measure up. The weight of early years of feeling rejected still kept me from liking what I saw in the mirror. My limited supply of self-esteem was regularly ravaged by the undeniable demands of four growing children.

I had nearly completed the manuscript over a period of

months. I had carefully scheduled each hour—practically each minute—to keep our four children loved and clean without giving up their special interests and activities. My husband continued to climb on airplanes with clean shirts and matched socks, Each week I faced our Bible study with pages of notes. But all that would change now. This "living sacrifice" (see Romans12:1), though nearly flattened by fatigue, still had enough energy to crawl down off the altar on its own.

"I'm quitting. Mark this chapter of my life closed. The end."

Though I wanted to cry for several more hours, the schedule would not permit it. The doorbell would ring any minute. Cold water splashed away the hot tears. A brisk towel rub evened the color off my face. Eye makeup camouflaged the puffiness. The hours rolled on, and so did the hurt. Hopefully, it didn't show on my face.

Instead of dealing with our hurts, we find many ways to run from them. I knew a man who ran away from his family by working seventy hours a week. His family needed the money, and the company depended on him. One woman immersed herself in soap operas. They were surely more exciting than her children, she reasoned. Another person joined every church committee. When his children got into trouble, his wife answered the phone and coped with the problems. We often try to ignore and avoid our problems, in an attempt to make them easier to live with.

In my crisis I found a comrade. How strange that an Egyptian slave named Hagar, more than three thousand years my senior, became special to me. In the past I had read quickly over her. (Why spend time studying a loser?) But now I hurt for her and with her. She obeyed her mistress, Sarah. She followed her marching orders. And she was mistreated. She reacted as I did to discouragement—she ran away.

Our running was different. Hagar was making her way through a desert, perhaps trying to return to Egypt. Being pregnant, she might well have been suffering discomfort. My running was well camouflaged. Only my husband knew that I'd declared I would quit. No more writing, speaking, and teaching Bible studies. I would run and remain in my comfortable, carpeted, secure home. I would avoid whatever hurt.

My running did not keep God from touching me through Hagar. Look what happened to her, as she fled from her mistress, Sarah.

> Now the angel of the LORD found her by a spring of water in the wilderness, by the spring on the way to Shur. And he said, "Hagar, Sarai's maid, where have you come from, and where are you going?" [Genesis 16:7-8]

That seemed strange. God knew where she had come from and where she was going. Why did He bother to ask? God was asking Hagar the question He asks of every person who runs away during hard times. He has asked it during every decade—not for His own benefit, but for ours.

"Miriam Neff, servant of Mine, where have you come from, and where are you going?"

"Lord, I was doing Your will, and it was to result in—"

"How could you know the result I have planned, daughter? A faithful servant is not to plan the outcome. That privilege belongs only to the Master. The Master has no obligation to tell the servant the strategy plans or share the overall blueprint.

"Why have you been faithful, daughter? Was it your whole-hearted response to Me? Was it because of your complete confidence in Me? Or was it because you saw your own objective being accomplished through your faithfulness?"

So that's where I had come from. I saw my past in a different perspective. My servant garb looked somewhat tattered. My utter dependence on the Lord was not so "utter" after all.

"Where are you going?" He continued.

I wonder if Moses heard those same words as he ran from Egypt (Exodus 2:15). Had he not murdered the Egyptian for fighting one of Moses' Hebrew brothers? Surely God approved of that. Surely that was part of Moses' marching orders. And what about Jonah? The ship headed to Tarshish was so convenient (Jonah 1:3). Didn't God perhaps provide it for him? Jonah felt so much peace about running away that he was able to sleep in the ship, even during a heavy storm.

Then there's Elijah. He ran after great victory. God may well have asked, "Where have you come from?" And Elijah might have answered, "From Mount Carmel where You proved Yourself to be trustworthy, O LORD." Instead he fled from the angry queen, Jezebel (1 Kings 19:3).

"It is enough now, O LORD," Elijah said before he went to sleep (1 Kings 19:4-5). Elijah echoed my own aching heart and perhaps yours when you are discouraged. I am learning some priceless lessons from the running Hagars, Moseses, Elijahs and Jonahs. Running away doesn't manage discouragement. They were allowed to run, but they were required to return. Moses returned to Egypt. It was forty years later, but he returned.

Jonah went to Nineveh. The transportation was unpleasant (possibly equally unpleasant for the fish), but he returned.

Elijah returned. Hagar returned. Maybe they are privileged to be recorded in Scripture because they were willing to return. God does not intend discouragement to become an embedded emotional habit. It may be a temporary holding pattern, but not a permanent landing place.

What happened to them? Their stories are different. The results in each case are unique. Moses returned to lead his Hebrew brothers and sisters out of Egypt. The wicked city of Nineveh was converted by Jonah's preaching. Elijah anointed his successor. Hagar's son was born into Sarah's household. In the uniqueness of each situation runs a common thread. "You may leave," whispers the Lord, "but only after completing the task as I have assigned it to you." With His firm, tender touch God began applying the lesson to me, His rebellious student.

The previous year I had chosen Job 23:14 as my verse for the year: "For he performeth the thing that is appointed for me: and many such things are with him" (KJV). Beware of selecting your verse for the year from the book of Job! I chose it in a state of excitement. I was anticipating a year jam-packed with blessing and brimming with miracles from God's overflowing storehouse. And He (God) was going to do the "performing." I would just float from one rose blossom to another. But my condition was a far cry from my dream. Disillusioned, I examined my verse in another translation.

"He carries out his decree against me, and many such plans he still has in store" (Job 23:14, NIV). My verse did not sound so appealing anymore. Then I looked at a third translation of the passage:

Behold, I go forward but He is not there,
And backward, but I cannot perceive Him;
When He acts on the left, I cannot behold Him;
He turns on the right, I cannot see Him.
But He knows the way I take;
When He has tried me, I shall come forth as gold.
My foot has held fast to His path;
I have kept His way and not turned aside.
I have not departed from the command of His lips;
I have treasured the words of His mouth more than my
    necessary food.
But He is unique and who can turn Him?
And what His soul desires, that He does.
For He performs what is appointed for me,
And many such decrees are with Him.
Therefore, I would be dismayed at His presence;
When I consider, I am terrified of Him.
It is God who has made my heart faint,
And the Almighty who has dismayed me,
But I am not silenced by the darkness,
Nor deep gloom which covers me"

Job 23:8-17

I was discouraged, because I felt God had let me down. He was
not working on my behalf. Wrong. I was running forward and
backward. He was working on the left and right. I could neither
see nor feel Him, but He knew the route I was taking. And even
in my running, it was God's intention that after all the huffing
and puffing, questioning and rebelling, tears and repentance, I
would come out shining like gold!

Job recognized that God stood alone. With all my plotting and
planning, God would not allow me to usurp His position of being
the decision-maker in my life. He was to take the steps, and I was
to follow in them, not run ahead. Job and I shared a common
misconception. We felt God had a decree against us. And what
human is not inclined to think that during a time of crisis? With
a stomach in knots, a splitting headache, or a throbbing neck, we
think that surely God's grace and love isn't smiling down on us!
How vital it is for us to continue daily opening His Word—even
though we ache, and our fingers almost refuse to turn the pages.

I'm sure that it did not "just happen" that my daily reading at
that time was in Judges.

> Now these are the nations which the LORD left, to test Israel
> by them (that is, all who had not experienced any of the
> wars of Canaan; only in order that the generations of the
> sons of Israel might be taught war, those who had not
> experienced it formerly). . . . And they were for testing
> Israel, to find out if they would obey the commandments of
> the LORD. . . . [Judges 3:1-2, 4]

God's loving decree for us was that we become battle-worthy.
He demands that we get into shape, though we cannot see what
will happen next week or next year. God has already made the
appointment, and He intends for us to be ready to meet it.

My phone had rung a few weeks before. "I hope someone takes
those tapes from your Bible study and chokes you with them!
What right do you have to teach?" A harsh non-identifiable
voice emptied her arsenal of anger on me and then hung up. My
mind began to scramble. Had I heard that voice before? What
right did that person have to intrude into my home and my
refuge—on my day off!

My fear and anger began to melt, as I imagined what kind of
person would make a phone call like that. *Poor soul. How messed
up, how insecure, how unhappy, she must be!* As the smoke of
overheated emotions cleared, the Lord had a lesson for me.
"Look closely into the faces of the people I send to the Bible
study that you've never seen before. Love them, even though
you don't know their burdens. They may more desperately need
your prayers than those who have the nerve to tell you where
they hurt. Do you care for them, too?"

Saturday's commotion at the Neff residence demanded that I
leave my quiet corner by the phone. Would our electrician friend
stay for lunch? Where is the baby? Oops, it's almost noon, and
our three-year-old is still shuffling about in his pj's. Can Valerie's
friend come over? My knees were no longer shaking. "Thank
You, Lord."

Here was another kind of battle experience—an opportunity
to choose to obey God. He always allows us options. He has
never delighted in robots who are programmed to do His will. If

God wanted that, He would not have created men and women who could choose to accept Him or reject Him.

To be willing to teach His Word in our weekly Bible study was a step I'd taken in childlike faith. I had not realized what a delight it would be to dig and study and expand my hours with the Lord. I also had not realized the burden of facing an unfamiliar and perhaps confusing passage about which many women would be expecting clear explanations and applications. I did not realize that as I dug into the Word, my own inadequacies and shortcomings would stand out in bold relief. I did not realize the personal burdens that many women would ask me to bear with them. Why did discouragement have to wrap every new opportunity for growth?

For the Christian, each week, each day, each minute provides another opportunity to choose between obedience and discouragement. We can declare with Job, perhaps with shaking voice, "But I am not silenced by the darkness, nor deep gloom which covers me"(Job 23:17).

My faith reaches out of the darkness to grasp what I cannot see. I will come out shining like gold, not because I see any gleaming light, but because God has gold in me that He is refining (see Isaiah 1:25). My feet want to be running away, but I will choose to stand. I want to echo David when he sang, "I run in the path of your commands, for you have set my heart free" and "I will walk about in freedom, for I have sought out your precepts" (Psalm 119:32, 45, NIV).

So you've responded to discouragement by quitting, by running away. How can you return? Facing the fact that you're running away is painfully necessary, and the trip back is not easy.

As Christians mistakenly pushed onto pedestals at times, it's hard to admit that we hurt, that we need help, that we are sinking instead of swimming. The feeling of aloneness is indeed a "deep gloom which covers me." In the healing process of returning, I was again taught by Moses, Elijah, Jonah, and Hagar.

Lesson 1—Timing *God's Timing is Always Right.*

Moses identified with his Jewish kinsmen rather than his adopted Egyptian family; that was God's will. But it was not God's will for Moses to decide when the Egyptians would free the

Jews. Our objectives may be right. Our marching orders from God may be right. But our timing may be wrong. Who can oppose God? We must live with His timing. Was Moses ready to lead the Jews out? What if an insurrection had occurred when he killed the Egyptian? God alone can see the spectrum and determine the proper time.

Perhaps you have felt, as I have, that you had to be the bionic Christian person. For me that meant total wife, perfect mother, overbooked teacher, hospitable homemaker, people helper, and five-times-weekly church attender. God does not desire a burned-out army. God's timing is based on what He created: the twenty-four hour day, men and women with two hands and two feet and bodies that require rest. Perhaps it is God's will for you to finish all you have begun, but not immediately. It has occurred to me that I will not be a living sacrifice if I kill myself in the process. *Don't get ahead of God. Be patient*

Lesson 2—Perspective *God's perspective*

If us is a Balance Tw Growth.

Elijah had lost his perspective when he ran away. He thought his were the only feet in God's army. He was alone in representing the Lord to his corrupt nation. The pressure was too great. God readied Elijah for the return trip. God had used Elijah in earth-shaking, attention-getting, mind-boggling ways before. And now Elijah had to be willing to be used in a quiet way. He had to anoint his successor. God got Elijah's attention with a rock-shattering wind, an earthquake, and fire. But then He spoke in a gentle whisper, "What are you doing here, Elijah?" (1 Kings 19:13b).

Good servants do not hide; nor do they write their own job descriptions. Elijah's perspective returned. God could work any way He pleased. Elijah was not alone. "Go back the way you came," God said. Elijah was willing to train his successor. It is hard to give up responsibility. Though we may complain about our tasks, we don't want to be replaced. "Faithful is He who calls you, and He also will bring it to pass" (1 Thessalonians 5:24). The "it" in this verse is God's refinement choice, not mine.

Lesson 3—Objective

I learn from Jonah that I can return and complete what God asked me to do in the first place. And the result can be successful for everyone but me. Jonah finished his task, but he was angry. He really wanted God to destroy Nineveh rather than to have compassion on the lost city. Poor Jonah! His feelings were hurt. He was not used in the way he wanted to be.

Paul said God counted him faithful in putting him into the ministry (1 Timothy 1:12). God evaluated what He saw in Paul and stamped him "usable." Paul accepted the challenge and privilege with faith and love. He proceeded with joy in spite of conflict that would send me scampering to Elijah's cave. Fatigue, hunger, threats, beatings, and shipwreck did not destroy Paul's vigor and joy in pursuing his objective.

Jonah acknowledged that God was a God of grace and love, but he did not accept it for himself and proceeded with a case of discouragement and depression. Nineveh was saved, but Jonah did not enjoy the blessing. His objective did not mesh with God's.

Lesson 4—Focus

I am more important than my ministry. I'm learning another lesson from Hagar's trip back home. Could it be that Hagar ran away for the sake of her unborn child? Being mistreated would not have been an uncommon lot for a slave. But did she perhaps decide that she would change the future of her unborn child? God had a lesson for her. "It's you I'm interested in today. I'll look out for the future. What is to happen through your son will be My objective." After Hagar's encounter with the angel of the Lord, she said, "Thou art a God who sees [me]" (Genesis 16:13). How could God work through me, if I had already determined how I wanted Him to use me? I was running away from what He wanted to do in me. The greater miracle is not the thousands who are reached through a faithful servant of God; it is how He shapes any human woman or man into a faithful servant of His.

Are you discouraged? Perhaps there is a person in your life that you feel you can tolerate no more. The person may be a co-worker, a husband or wife, a fussy two-year-old, or a teenage son or daughter. You have resolved to cut off the relationship. Has your ministry left you dry? Feeding the flock has left your storehouse empty, and you are starving. Perhaps you are locked into circumstances that allow no room for satisfying needs that are vital to your emotional survival. Stop and consider that what you see as failure may be God's compliment to you, as He refines your character. Perhaps He is saying, "The gold in you is too precious to remain unpolished." God doesn't shape masses and direct history by neglecting individuals.

Consider that perhaps He is bringing your perspective around to mesh with His. His objective is to refine you, but His method may be different from the one you had in mind. It is likely that His objective encompasses much more than you had in mind.

Consider that your running away does not tie God's hands. His timing is right; His perspective is balanced; His objective is clear. And His focus is you.

Steps to Take

1. Maintain the habit of reading the Bible. Perspective doesn't come from looking at circumstances or other people. Perspective comes from focusing on God. We do this by habitually reading His Word—all of it—the Old and New Testaments. I reach for it in confidence, in desperation, and when I do not feel like reading. I have read to find answers and have been loved so completely that my question did not matter. Through His Word, we are able to hope when we do not see immediate results. We become better acquainted with His goals and see that His results are worth waiting for.

2. Keep encouraging reminders around you. I have a friend who always wears a butterfly. It may be a ring, stick pin, or design on her clothing. It reminds her that God has been changing her in positive ways. These things are not like rabbit's feet that we depend on for success; they have no power of themselves. They are just reminders that encourage us.

3. Encourage other people. Being part of their solution rather than their problem encourages you, too. "But encourage one another day after day, as long as it is still called 'Today,' lest any one of you be hardened by the deceitfulness of sin" (Hebrews 3:13). A lady in our Bible class piped up with a humorous remark that had us rolling with laughter. I called the pastor that afternoon to pass the incident on. How

delightful to hear him laugh! The phone conversation probably took two minutes from his busy schedule, but it lightened his burdens a little. Keep laughter in your life. Share it with others when you can.

Often we discover that we have not laughed for too long. One expecially dismal Chicago winter my husband outfitted our family with ice skates, and everyone took to the ice. The children learned like candidates for the Olympics. That was fortunate, because they had to keep their wobbling, scrambling mother up on her feet. It was a good cure for the discouragement of cabin fever.

4. Take a few hours, or a day, and change your routine. Discouragement often accompanies being totally engrossed with the immediate problem. Routine good habits facilitate efficient, productive living, but sometimes they keep us from getting new perspectives on problems.

Even Jesus needed to get away from the demands of His ministry. He absorbed the rugged beauty of the wilderness or sea. Naturally we need change also.

Hear, O Lord, when I cry with my voice,
And be gracious to me and answer me.
When Thou didst say, "Seek My face," my heart said
    to Thee,
"Thy face, O Lord, I shall seek."
Do not hide Thy face from me,
Do not turn Thy servant away in anger;
Thou hast been my help;
Do not abandon me nor forsake me,
O God of my salvation!
For my father and my mother have forsaken me,
But the Lord will take me up.
Teach me Thy way, O Lord,
And lead me in a level path,
Because of my foes.
Do not deliver me over to the desire of my adversaries;
For false witnesses have risen against me,
And such as breathe out violence.
I would have despaired unless I had believed

That I would see the goodness of the LORD
In the land of the living.
Wait for the LORD;
Be strong, and let your heart take courage;
Yes, wait for the LORD.

Psalm 27:7-14

10

Depression

Have you ever thought of depression as being good? Until recently, I considered it one of those bad emotions that just happen to people. I thought that, since we Christians have God's power available to us, we could pull ourselves up by our bootstraps. If we were depressed, we could go through steps a, b, and c—thinking positively, getting outside, and being thankful —and become happy again.

If this formula didn't work, our depression probably resulted from sin that we were not willing to give up. God would keep pressing the depression button until we yelled, "Uncle!" From what I'd read, this depression always grew from a repressed or frozen anger. The solution to this depression was to ask forgiveness and stop being angry.

Some cases of depression may fit that formula, but most do not. By insisting on those two solutions to depression, we guarantee that many people will continue to suffer, and many Christians will go to the wrong places looking for other solutions or at least relief from their pain.

The word *depression* means different things to different people. Psychologists and medical doctors use definitions that include observable symptoms. They speak of clinical depression, in which feelings have become so intense that physiological symptoms become evident. Most agree, however, that depression is a great masquerader. A person can be depressed and not experience any of the common symptoms. I use the word with its common meaning, as the feeling that goes beyond temporary discouragement.

Emotional pain results in physiological symptoms. Anger, guilt, or grief feelings may be involved, but a sense of worthlessness and helplessness overpowers a person. When the wounds are deep, and depression has become a way of life, some beautiful biblical truths are necessary for healing and for the management of depression.

First of all, we need to acknowledge the fact that depression is a normal way for our emotions to deal with trauma in our lives. Being depressed is not a sin. This may be a new thought to you. Compare depression with anger in this light. Remember, Jesus was angry, but He did not sin. He reacted to certain events with anger. His anger energized Him to respond properly to those events. Like anger, depression becomes sin only when we respond in the wrong way or become depressed for the wrong reasons. According to Cohen and Gans, in *The Other Generation Gap,* * depression can be the most logical and appropriate reaction a person experiences in a loss. It can serve a positive, healthy purpose for people confronted with immediate problems.

Let me illustrate. A thirty-five-year-old woman wakes up dreading the day. For years she has been energetic, outgoing, and productive. Now her head has a dull ache that aspirin won't touch. She dreads the day, because she is sure that nothing good will happen. She dreads the night, with its long, lonely hours of wondering if sleep will come to relieve her painful thoughts. Weeks are filled with uncontrollable crying. She is afraid of her former activities. What if she begins to cry in a store or with a group of her friends? She can't understand or explain what is happening, so she isolates herself.

This woman illustrates the main symptoms of depression. According to Minirth and Meyer, these symptoms carry the labels of:

1. moodiness (or sadness)
2. painful thinking (negative thoughts about self, lack of motivation, indecision)
3. physical symptoms of sleeplessness and loss of appetite
4. anxiety resulting in irritability

* Steven Cohen and Bruce Gans, *The Other Generation Gap: You and Your Aging Parents* (New York, N.Y.: Warner Books, 1980).

5. delusional thinking, or being out of touch with reality (pp. 23-28).

Traumatic events do happen in the lives of Christians. The resulting depression should first be labeled normal, not sin. Sometimes the resulting depression is mild. You may have experienced the symptoms of depression over the loss of a job, a serious drop in income, or the death of a friend or relative. I have friends who have experienced divorce, paralysis from an injury, and the loss of a mate after a long, God-honoring, intimate marriage. These women all experienced more than mild depression.

Many of us face depression at certain times—even without such traumatic experiences. I am the woman described earlier, who dreaded the day. It is unrealistic to say that believers should never experience depression. They did in the days of Elijah and Moses, and they still do today.

Philip Yancey makes an applicable point in *Where Is God When It Hurts?** Physical pain has a good purpose. It warns us about injury or disease. If a person cannot feel pain, she is in trouble. If, for example, because of leprosy a person has no feeling in his feet, he may wear shoes that rub until parts of his feet are gone. This could have been prevented, if pressure had been taken off that weakened part of the body—if it had been protected. Instead, the damage is irreparable.

Depression warns us that we have a rub or hurt somewhere. Sometimes it is expressed through obvious responses, like grief. The death of a mate or child shakes us. We stagger while adjusting to our loss. Accompanying depression may go unrecognized. Our feelings and actions baffle us. They may be so complex that we become annoyed, or even distressed, trying to figure out the how and why of what is happening to us.

In my own experience, my mind and emotions were struggling to mend themselves. My emotions had been crippled by experiences from my childhood, although I was not aware of the injury for years. During my depression, my mind dredged up painful memories that had long been forgotten. I felt anger, hatred, and

---

* Philip Yancey, *Where Is God When It Hurts?* (Grand Rapids: Zondervan, 1977).

guilt. I did not realize that my mind had to acknowledge the injury in order for healing to begin.

Our minds strive to heal the injuries, just as our bodies strive to recover from illness. Sometimes we can identify the event that triggered our depression. Sometimes we can't. sometimes a seemingly insignificant incident touches off a wholly unpredictable, profound depression. If we have viewed ourselves as well-balanced and emotionally strong (as I did), this is especially disturbing.

Physical healing is work The body must mend, and it may require some assistance for the job: vitamins, minerals, protein, rest, and perhaps even antibiotics. The body needs time to assimilate those. Emotional and mental healing through depression is also work. That is perhaps why this emotion is so difficult to live with and to manage. We want quick and easy answers to everything. The roots of depression grow over many years. Immediate results are negative. The positive fruit is produced only after a long period of time.

As I write this, I see a lovely Jerusalem cherry plant next to my writing table. The plump, red fruit hangs in contrast to the lush, green leaves. A month ago, this beautiful plant was covered with miserable-looking blossoms. I couldn't avoid the acrid smell or appreciate the beauty of the foliage. The plant looked ugly, and it smelled even worse. But it would have no beauty now if it had not first grown through that cycle.

Depression is like that. The depression period of my life was miserable. But I had to experience it for healing to occur. Would I have asked for the events that led to my depression? No way. Did I enjoy the feelings of those months? Absolutely not. But now I am glad and thankful for the experience—and so is my husband! The result of depression has been good. the work of emotional and mental healing has been productive.

Certain tools can help us in the healing process of depression. But before grabbing the tools, a word of caution is necessary: Beware of taking to heart all the advice of friends. Remember Job's experience. We have said that depression is complex. Its roots are deep. Perhaps no one will really understand your case. Here are three pieces of advice I received from friends: "You are neglecting your husband"; "You are neglecting your children"; "You are neglecting yourself." Listening to all of the advice I was getting was only more depressing! Be careful. Not everyone who cares about you can help you.

Tools for Healing Depression

TOOL NUMBER 1: A POSITIVE SELF-IMAGE

Much of the emotional pain we experience during depression stems from a lack of self-worth. Dr. David D. Burns, author of *Feeling Good: The New Mood Therapy*, says that only your own sense of self-worth determines how you feel.* I have the right and obligation to see myself positively, as God sees me. I can adopt His image of me as my own or destroy myself, using some other basis for self-worth.

There once was a man who had everything going for him. People looked twice at his height and good looks when he walked by. When he was a young man, God chose him to be a leader. Maybe it was because he was a strong, hard worker. Maybe it was because he was not conceited. Whatever the reason, God saw his potential and gave him the highest political position of leader-ship in the country, making him king of Israel.

God never gives us an assignment that He cannot enable us to handle; this was true in this young man's case as well. In fact, this man was given special reassurance. ". . . do . . . what the occasion requires; for God is with you" (1 Samuel 10:7).

The world began to spin. The people from his hometown became jealous of him. (Newly acquired clout usually divides our friends and multiplies our acquaintances.) Before long, military threats were followed by victories. His political and military stature grew. He did not accumulate women, as many men do while gaining in popularity. He had one wife and five children. At least one of his sons grew up to become a man of integrity and great ability.

After a few years, clouds of depression immobilized him. He was unable to sleep. He plotted to kill a man who had served him faithfully. In anger he even tried to kill his own son. He spent his last years filled with hatred and bitterly pursued a man who had vowed never to harm him.

* David D. Burns, *Feeling Good: The New Mood Therapy* (New York, N.Y.: Morrow, 1980).

Why did our all-wise God include the story of Saul in the Bible? There is beautiful wisdom about depression in his experience. As we read of Saul's beginnings, we see that he was a humble person. He was surprised to be anointed king, because he came from a small clan—the tribe of Benjamin. When it came time for his public appointment, he hid. This certainly does not picture a man who was seeking recognition or glorying in his heritage. After Saul assumed his position of king, we still find him working in the fields as he had done before. Saul's humility was a characteristic God wanted to use.

In Saul's early reign, we see that he had another valuable characteristic; he did not hold grudges. In that day, a new king received gifts. Some troublemakers from his hometown responded to his kingship, saying, "How can this one deliver us?" (1 Samuel 10:27a). They despised him and brought him no gifts. But Saul kept silent; he already had a circle of valiant men. He could have extorted gifts or made the troublemakers uncomfortable in many ways. But he didn't. You can tell a person's stature by the people he ignores.

After Saul's first great military victory, in the frenzy of celebration and the loyalty of success, the people wanted to kill all who had opposed Saul's appointment as king, It would have been politically acceptable for Saul to give the nod of approval. He did not.

Saul had another characteristic God intended to use; he was a peacemaker. Saul became king of a group of people who were independent. They were divided by clans, and it was not their natural inclination to work together. Saul unified them. The scattered people who could be bullied by almost anyone became a nation of military might.

These very strengths, the characteristics that God most wanted to use, became twisted and distorted, knotted and misused. Depression was woven into the fabric of Saul's emotions. Saul did not work through his depression. He allowed it to become a negative, strangling emotion that changed his thinking, his living, and his patterns of behavior.

What happened to Saul's humility, his forgiving nature, and his ability to unify people? He succumbed to an identity crisis. He was special in the beginning for a God-given reason. God had created him and given him a job to do. He could have felt good about himself if he had accepted God's approval. But he began to seek man's approval instead.

This is most clearly seen in the way Saul reacted to victory. When he was humble he said, ". . . this day the Lord has rescued Israel" (1 Samuel 11:13, NIV). As he grabbed for more, he took the glory of victory for himself. He robbed his own son of credit for attacking a Philistine garrison. When other soldiers won honor in battle, Saul was jealous. ". . . Saul has slain his thousands, and David his ten thousands" (1 Samuel 18:7b). Saul eyed David from that day on, and the acrid atmosphere of depression surrounded him, affecting the whole nation.

Saul is a classic example of a person who could have had a positive self-concept. But when his crisis time came, he looked for people-approval, and that is never enough to give a person a positive self-image. Healthy emotional balance cannot coexist with self-centered, "I-must-look-like-the-greatest" behavior. When we take our need for approval to God, He accepts, loves, and supports us. When we take our need for approval to other people, they cannot love us enough, show us enough acceptance, or give us a basis for worth. We then become angry inside and may even hold grudges against those who did not satisfy us. People simply cannot do what God can do; they cannot supply unqualified acceptance.

Saul began to make mistakes; like chain reactions, they linked him with growing, internal guilt. He refused to change his behavior, so the guilt surfaced in destruction. He foolishly bound his soldiers in an oath to fast when they needed energy. Perhaps he reveled in their loyal obedience at the time, but later he had to scramble to cope with the sin that resulted. He caught his own son in the net. He did not completely obey God and destroy a nation he defeated; instead, he saved what looked good to him. Possessions became important to him. He lost his ability to overlook wrongs and offenses. People held more power over him than God did. Look at one of Saul's confessions. "I have sinned; I have indeed transgressed the command of the LORD and your words, because I feared the people and listened to their voice" (1 Samuel 15:24).

Samuel told Saul that a new king would be selected, because Saul had rejected the Lord. Saul should have fallen on the ground and wept at his great failure. How did he respond? "I have sinned; but please honor me now before the elders of my people and before Israel . . ." (1 Samuel 15:30a). The grudges nurtured by Saul's twisted self-image resulted in irresponsible action. And the guilt over those actions added to the weight of his depression.

Have you examined yourself to see if your depression cannot heal because of a twisted self-image? Sometimes we feel so worthless, so messed up, and so disgusted with ourselves or our sin that we feel we are nobody. Remember, you are created and loved as a special being that God delights in. The very weakness you have discovered in dissecting your depression may be what God wants to use for His glory.

Tool Number 2: A Healthy Body

We have said that depression is often triggered by a traumatic event in our lives. Post-partum blues is the term for the depression that often follows giving birth to a baby. Our bodies have exerted the greatest effort ever in the least amount of time in our lives. We often feel conflict over the addition of another dependent being.

Recent books about mid-life crises point out that depression accompanies the realization that our lives are half over, and we still have unfulfilled dreams. We discover that our bodies cannot maintain their former paces. Our appearances or shapes may be changing, and we don't like what we see. We want to work harder and exercise, too.

Depression accompanies low blood sugar, whether it is continual or those temporary times of hunger before meals. It may follow a time when we've been especially busy.

What is a common denominator in all these situations? Our bodies are drained by a traumatic event, physical exertion, or both. Elijah exemplified this. He had experienced great victory. The emotional high of victory, though exhilarating to the mind and emotions, is demanding on the body. Elijah was threatened and ran away. His flight resulted in exhaustion accompanied by depression. God didn't grab his shoulder and rebuke him for his sinful emotion. He fed him. He let him rest. Then God was able to teach him another lesson. But first his body had to be restored.

A young mother may be especially susceptible to depression.

There are valid reasons for this. Pregnancy and a nursing child make demands on the body. In our "skinny" culture, she is probably trying to keep her weight down at the expense of her general health. Her sleep pattern is disrupted by her infant's demands. If she has other small children, it is especially difficult for her to get enough rest. She is probably struggling with her identity at the same time, since the feminist movement has so devalued motherhood. Eating habits that sustained her before marriage and motherhood are not adequate now. Sleep habits that sustained her when there were not constant emotional drains from small children are no longer possible or sufficient. Since demands on her time have increased, she may be more likely to reach for quick sugar pick-me-ups and a cup of black coffee, instead of taking time to eat a piece of fruit.

It's good to remember that God values the bodies He gave us. As temples of His Holy Spirit, they are important. As His creative masterpieces, they are important. Caring for our bodies is a part of our stewardship. We don't get the best mileage from our cars by running them with no thought of their state of repair. I found myself running my body like a bucket of bolts. As long as I could get it going, it was full speed ahead. Collapse was inevitable.

Graciously, God put Mrs. Opal Fasig in my life. At seventy-five, her complexion was clearer than mine. She was active and vibrant. She explained different vitamins and told me where I could buy the best for the least. She was an example of wise eating habits, of good stewardship of her body.

Jim Conway points out in his book *Men In Mid-Life Crisis* that exercise and being outdoors helped him through his time of depression.* When you are depressed, it is unwise to plan a program of rigorous exercise to get your sagging body back in shape. Implementing the program would probably be impossible. But it may be reasonable to begin taking walks. I found that biking was therapeutic. Getting into a nearby forest preserve was soothing and good exercise at the same time. The river eased hurts from my mind and rolled them downstream. The earthy smell of woods crowded out pressures. Others may see the Des

---

* Jim Conway, *Men in Mid-Life Crisis* (Elgin, Ill.: David C. Cook, 1978).

Plaines River as dying and polluted, but it's the only river I have. It has been a haven for ducks and for my muddled thinking.

Depression can have some good results—changed habits that benefit your body. Now I take bike trips to the forest preserve out of desire, not desperation. The exercise is still good; the therapy is inexpensive; and the result is satisfying.

TOOL NUMBER 3: EDITED AUTOMATIC THOUGHTS

Perhaps you think you have a one-track mind. Nobody does. We may not be aware of what is going on in our minds, but many tracks are humming.

For example, someone pays you a compliment. "You look pretty tonight." You mumble that you hardly had time to get dressed. You borrowed the skirt from your daughter, and it doesn't fit right. "Congratulations, you've done a nice piece of work." You tell them you were just lucky; someone else could have done better. On a back track of your mind a message is humming. "I'm dumb and ugly. I'm dumb and ugly. Compliments can't be true. I'm dumb and ugly."

Though we are not consciously aware of this thought pattern, it is powerfully effective. Everything we see and hear is reinterpreted through these automatic thoughts.

During times of depression, these thoughts are louder and more numerous than usual. Common automatic thoughts of the depressed person are: "I'm no good." "It was so stupid of me to do that. Now nobody will like me." "People don't treat me right." During depression these automatic thoughts may monopolize our minds, although we may not even be aware of it. However, thoughts affect our feelings and we are very aware of the feelings. We feel like nobodies. We feel guilty. We feel conflict.

What do we do about those thoughts? First, we snag them and identify them. And then we edit them. We correct them if they are wrong, and throw them out if they are useless.

Pat felt like a nobody. But as long as she was accomplishing something, she could live with the feeling. She went to school, held a good job, married, and had six children. When her last child was three, her life nosedived into depression. Her friends lectured her on the successes in her life. "Look at these fine, healthy children. Your husband provides for you and is a caring man. Remember your degrees." Pat then felt guilty for feeling depressed.

She asked herself, "Why do I feel like a nobody?" She thought of her childhood. Her mother had died when she was seven. Her father had been indifferent. She had always been able to attract her stepmother's and father's attention by achievement. It became vital to her surface feeling of self-worth to be accomplishing something. When she had no measurable accomplishments, she felt worthless.

Pat snagged the automatic thought, "I'm a nobody unless I'm accomplishing something measurable." She edited it. "I *feel* like a nobody because of my past. I *am* somebody to God, because He made me and has a plan for my life. He accepts me whether I am accomplishing measurable things or not." Pat's feelings about herself, now based on facts, began to change.

Such realizations do not occur instantly. Sometimes professional help is required to capture those subconscious, automatic thoughts. It is worth the investment, because the feelings will not change until we base them on the correct facts.

During depression it is common for our inner thoughts to become irrational. We make a mistake. We exaggerate it. After a fender-bender, I conclude that I'm the worst driver in the world. I spill something as simple as water and browbeat myself for not being careful. An investment depreciates, and I label myself a failure. It is important for us to interpret these thoughts and label them accurately. We do make mistakes; everybody does. It's part of living and learning.

It may be helpful to write your thoughts down. Editing may be easier on paper. Philippians 4:8 gives us guidelines for editing those thoughts. Are they true, honest, and just? Are they pure, lovely, and of good report? Is there any virtue that will come from keeping that thought? If not, throw it out.

The Bible teaches us that what a man or woman thinks in his or her heart is what he or she will become (Proverbs 23:7). Also, it teaches us that what we think in our hearts will guide our tongues (Luke 8:45). If we do not catch and edit wrong thoughts, they will mold us and affect all our relationships. If we think that we're dumb and ugly long enough, eventually we'll begin to act dumb and ugly. If we think people treat us unfairly, eventually we will make them treat us that way. Then there will be no positive fruit from the period of depression. It can remain a bad emotional habit that carries misery along with it.

TOOL NUMBER 4: A SYMPATHETIC FRIEND

"A [woman] of many friends comes to ruin, but there is a friend who sticks closer than a [sister]" (Proverbs 18:24). Friends can intensify the pain of depression. As I said earlier, not everyone who cares about you can help you. Friends often don't understand. Sometimes the level of their caring is superficial. However, you may discover a true gem among your friendships during depression.

A helping friend will sympathize with you, while gently helping you up, instead of accompanying you down the tubes. This is a rare-faceted friendship.

Please sympathize with your own friend. If her case is anything like mine, remember that her pain is real and usually justified. One woman went to her prayer circle hurting. She had been battling depression for weeks and felt she was ready to go over the edge. She told her friends she was hurting. They wouldn't believe her. How could there be hurt behind her beautiful face? They thought she had the perfect family. They refused her plea for help.

She found comfort for her pain in a bottle. She didn't have to keep explaining and convincing to get warmth and numbness. The bottle was guaranteed, always available relief.

What do you do when a friend gets sick? We say we're sorry. If she's in the hospital, we bring her perfume or chocolates or lilacs from our garden. That's sympathy.

When my friend Gail was paralyzed from the waist down by an accident, she received letters saying that if she had more faith, she could get up and walk. Another letter said if she would dig out the sin in her life and repent, she would be healed. That is not sympathy or friendship.

A man in the Bible had the same problem Gail did, though his handicap was different. He had been blind since birth. People asked Jesus, "Who sinned, this man or his parents?" (John 9:2).

Jesus answered in effect, "Neither. It happened so that I could teach you judgmental, coldhearted people a lesson" The lesson Jesus taught by His action was that He came to earth to help hurting people become whole. He came to face their handicap, rather than deny it existed or deny that they had a legitimate hurt. Only then could healing take place.

Depression is a hurt as real as a fist in the stomach. Is it wrong to say, "I'm sorry you're hurting," "Your parents shouldn't have treated you that way," or "You must really miss him at night"? Sympathy is holding each other and crying over the human things that happen. It is loving a crumbling person and giving her room to crumble. It's staying there to hold the pieces, whether you can help to put them together again or not.

That kind of friendship is rare, isn't it? If you have it, you may not need the next tool.

Tool Number 5: Professional Christian Help

Not everyone needs professional Christian help during times of depression. But sometimes we do. I have heard Christians say that a Christian should never need a psychiatrist. But those same people will hurry off to the doctor for an antibiotic if they have an infection. They will have casts put on their broken arms to aid proper healing.

I will not discuss the issue at length here. I think it is necessary, however, for us to realize that our minds and emotions are complex. Sometimes we are unable to unravel painful tangles alone. Many times our friends and families cannot be objective enough to help. Sometimes they are even part of the problem.

It is my opinion that the help of a non-Christian professional is extremely limited. The non-Christian is seriously handicapped in helping us to establish feelings of self-worth. Our whole basis for self-esteem originates from God. He made us uniquely in His image, and He accepts us as we are. If we erase God from the picture, we are beings that happened by accident. We have no purpose in life other than the goals we have set for ourselves. These will be selfish at best, but more likely destructive to ourselves and to others. Without God as the foundation, how can any self-esteem be established? Jesus is our flesh-and-blood example of God. His death for us proves our worth to Him and His Father. Now we have historical proof of our worth. I don't see how a healthy self-image can be established or reaffirmed without that biblical basis.

Methods used in secular counseling have become entwined with secular humanistic philosophy. Practices have become professionally acceptable that violate biblical principles. One Christian psychiatrist told of non-Christian colleagues who had intercourse with female patients to free them from the "hangup" of belonging to only one man. I have a friend whose teenage daughter was hospitalized and assigned to a bedroom of both young men and women. She was encouraged to form intimate relationships with everyone so she would feel accepted. Six months and $24,000.00 later, she was released with "no marked improvement."

Fortunately, today we do have well-qualified professionals who are Christians. Some professionals use the word "Christian" to attract a broader number of clients, but their practices are not biblical. Check not only the credentials but also the record and practices before you entrust your tangled emotions to someone for unraveling.

TOOL NUMBER 6: THANKFULNESS

We speak of this tool so glibly that it sounds generic. It is neither low cost nor low value, but a precious must in the positive work of depression. Since depression often follows traumatic events, we may want to accuse God rather than thank Him for whatever has happened. We can be sorry that the event happened, and we can visualize or dream of what might have been if circumstances had been different.

Eventually, if we are to allow depression to work positively, we must apply the Romans 8:28 principle. God is big enough and powerful enough to bring good out of anything. This fact has enabled Corrie Ten Boom to thank God for her years in a concentration camp. This fact enabled Paul to write a positive letter of praise to the Philippians. This fact has enabled Pat to thank God for her father and stepmother. I have been able to thank God for my childhood experiences. Thankfulness is acting on fact before our feelings have changed. Eventually you will feel thankful.

The Bible has always told us to be thankful. Since we are to give thanks always, we must develop the habit of thankfulness. Interestingly, secular research is just now "proving" this. In

Cognitive Therapy and the Emotional Disorders, Dr. Aaron T. Beck affirms that our moods don't decree our thoughts; our thoughts govern our moods.* If we think right, we'll feel right.

Do you want to *feel* thankful? Then *think* thankful. Make a list of what you can be thankful for. Review these benefits in your mind. Thank God out loud for them. Imagine different good things that might result from some of your painful, growing experiences. Thank God for the endless potential positives.

Steps to Take

1. Write down the basis for a positive self image. Write down what God thinks of you. Ephesians 1:2-8 may help you.
2. What realistic changes could you make in your eating habits? What activity would fit into your life for enjoyment and better health? Your body is worth the investment of planning and time.
3. Practice editing your subconscious, automatic thoughts. Memorize Philippians 4:8. An honest evaluation of yourself (Romans 12:3) includes your strengths. What qualities do you have that are available for God to use?
4. Be a sympathetic friend. If you have such a friend, treasure her.
5. What good might come from this growing time? Begin to thank God for the potential you may not see at the time. Someone else may be able to point it out, or you may eventually discover it yourself. Begin by thanking Him even before you see results.

Hear my prayer, O LORD!
And let my cry for help come to Thee.
Do not hide Thy face from me in the day of my distress;
Incline Thine ear to me;
In the day when I call answer me quickly.
For my days have been consumed in smoke,
And my bones have been scorched like a hearth.

* Aaron T. Beck, *Cognitive Therapy and the Emotional Disorders* (New York, N.Y.: New American Library, 1979).

My heart has been smitten like grass and withered away,
Indeed, I forget to eat my bread.

Psalm 102:1-4

Bless the LORD, O my soul;
And all that is within me, bless His holy name.
Bless the LORD, O my soul,
And forget none of His benefits;
Who pardons all your iniquities;
Who heals all your diseases;
Who redeems your life from the pit;
Who crowns you with loving kindness and compassion;
Who satisfies your years with good things,
So that your youth is renewed like the eagle.

Psalm 103:1-5

11
Grief

Could this woman be my mother? The eyes studying my face looked dull and gray instead of soft hazel. There was no twinkle of recognition yet. Except for the high cheek bones and a little russet-colored hair, she could have been another woman. Three years of cancer, chemotherapy, and cobalt treatments had destroyed Mama as I knew her.

Grief was for people who had lost a loved one. Mama was still here. I could stroke her face, smooth her gown, talk to her. Then why this pain? Why the anger at all the machinery around her; why the overwhelming feeling of being lost? To me, Mama was already gone. But I didn't have the right to grieve yet. Mama was still alive.

Perhaps in this lies the reason we (and I include myself) have such a struggle managing grief. We have spelled out the circumstances in which a person can legitimately feel grief. Many times life doesn't fit those prescribed circumstances.

An adult child grieves when she realizes she can never communicate with her parent on an adult level. By the time that parent dies, there is nothing left to grieve about; the relationship ended long ago. The tears are dried; the hurt has run its course. There's no more sorrow to cause literal pain. We make room for the person's grief whose parent has died. But we don't understand, and we are unresponsive to the person grieving over the end of a relationship.

We expect the divorcée to go through a period of grief. Expectations have died. Hope for that "happily ever after" is lost in bills for lawyers, questioning children, financial pressures, and lonely night hours.

113

But what about the person who begins to realize that there has been an emotional divorce in her marriage? They still share the same address, the same refrigerator, the same children, and the same bed, but the "together" is gone. Talking doesn't penetrate an invisible barrier; there's no transparency. Part of each of them is on the reserve shelf. This woman experiences grief, too.

Parents grieve when their child dies. But what do we call the hurt a parent experiences when their child brings the police to the front door? How do we label the feelings of the parent whose child has run away? What about the child who is tragically immobilized? What does a parent feel as she looks at her twenty-five-year-old son, who is unable to lift his hand to blow his own nose? That is also grief.

A man has loved another woman. "Triangles," they are called. He chooses to walk away from the relationship and try to salvage his marriage. He grieves. If the relationship has been an extended one, the grief is deep. Determination to commit himself completely to the marriage does not immediately erase the grasp of the other relationship on his life. "He deserves it," someone whispers. Regardless of others' judgments, the grief is still real. Whether grief comes due to our sin or in our innocence, it is still grief, and the hurt is still there. Grief brought on by sin often becomes more intense, because it must be faced alone with the additional hurt of guilt.

Grief has been defined as the slow and gradual adaptation to sudden and absolute separation from a loved one. I think we should expand the definition. Grief is experienced when we must adapt to separation from any person who is important to us, or to an extreme change in a person or relationship that has been a meaningful part of our life.

We experience grief for myriad reasons. Regardless of the cause, the mind and body always face intense pain. Like an army officer calling out the ranks, grief usually brings with it a batallion of other emotions—anxiety, hostility, guilt, loneliness, and depression.

Grief is not evil. It hurts; it is unwelcome. We would prefer to live without it. But none of us has that option. Just as life is always followed by death, so forming a relationship brings the potential for separation. Action is accompanied by risks. Grief could not be a bad emotion. Jesus experienced it. The Holy Spirit experiences it.

Jesus grieved at the hardness of men's hearts. Mark 3:5 tells us that His grief was accompanied by anger. Jesus hurt inside when He saw that the scribes and the Pharisees were more concerned with their rules than with people who were hurting. We are not alone in our experience. He feels with us.

Much that has been written on grief divides this emotion into stages. One author says there are three stages, another five, and another ten. Some put elements of time on each stage. After much reading, talking to many people, and examining my own experiences, I have chosen to see grief as a process rather than a series of stages. It seems dangerous to assign months or years to the process, because we are all so different.

I had read that losing one's mate through death was followed by a crisis stage that lasted for two or three weeks. As I talked to one widow, she described the numbness she felt after her husband died, For two months she felt nothing. She had loved her husband, but she felt nothing. Then the crisis came; then the hurt, the tears, and the anguish moved in. She experienced depression two years later, although some say that grieving should be complete in a little over a year.

It is dangerous for us to assign specific behaviors and time periods to grief, because we expect others and ourselves to fit the mold. Why does grief vary so much from person to person? It makes it hard for us to help each other. We think that telling others our experiences will help. But they can't identify at all. We have a hard time communicating because of all the differences.

The boundaries of grief are set by many variables. One of the most important is how much we valued the person or object we have lost. We grieve when the moving van pulls away with our friends, but that grief does not compare to the grief as we see a loved one's casket with mounds of dirt around it. The gentle beauty of flowers does not wipe out the darkness of that dark hole in the ground.

Grief that follows divorce can be traumatic. Some people reestablish productive lives within months; others still struggle years later.

Men grieve over losing a job. This is not socially acceptable, but it is a reality. If the job was rewarding, grief may be severe. Retirement can bring grief that receives little attention. In our culture, a man's job is an important part of his identity and existence. When that is taken away, he grieves. Since we often do not acknowledge this grief, he doesn't have the encouragement and help to work through his grief.

Mortality rates for men are especially high during the first year after retirement. Grief is a stressful event. Physical illnesses increase during grief. These range from common colds to cancer and heart attacks. Body reserves are involved in the work of grief rather than fighting disease.

Since the intensity of grief is related to how much we value what we have lost, we can see why losing a lifetime mate is probably the most intense grief we will suffer. Our expectations determine another variable in grief. We don't expect our children to leave us or die before we do. We expect them to grow with us and to be a part of our lives. Suicide of someone close to us—our mate or our child—is especially devastating, and partly for this reason. Knowing that we are about to lose someone does not erase the grief. But sometimes we begin our grief early work when we know separation is coming. Then we have our feet planted more firmly on the ground when the blow comes.

Another variable for the intensity of grief is how we've faced trauma and change in the past. Grief is hard work. It is giving up emotional dependence on what we no longer have. I have often been told that time is the healer for grief. I disagree. Healing depends on what happens during that time. Is the work of grief being completed? Working out our grief in a short period of time does not mean we've done it successfully. Success is integrating the loss into our lives and finding new resources with our dependence. Reordering our lives, not around the void, but out of it, is part of the work. Our track record of dealing with crisis—how we've faced change—is an indicator of how we'll manage grief.

What helps us with our grief-work? People can help in some areas, but others must be faced alone. Before the crisis comes, it is helpful to internalize the truth that grief is a normal process. The results of grieving can be positive. If we know that our experience of grief will be different from anyone else's, we will be less perplexed by our feelings and reactions.

Tears are part of the healing process. Don't be afraid to shed tears—buckets of them. They can't be forced, and they shouldn't be held back when they come. My Aunt Audrey's kitchen table has been my crying corner as I've watched Mama change. Living just down the street from her, my aunt is aware of Mama's daily routine and yet understands the shock we sisters struggle with, coming in tired after a long drive and wrestling to face a silent home with a hospital bed and no homemade goodies.

A misunderstanding of 1 Thessalonians 4:13 has given tears a bad reputation. We are taught that we should "not grieve, as do the rest who have no hope." This does not mean we should not cry—only that we are not without hope. Sometimes grieving people are admonished not to cry. "He is in heaven now. Isn't it wonderful—to think of him with Jesus?" That may be true. But we are hurting! Present with the Lord means absent from us! Our grief does not have the utter despondence of the person who believes everything is completely, utterly over. But we still feel the void that can be filled by nothing or no one.

God gives us tears to express this physical and emotional pain. "Jesus wept" (John 11:35). David graphically describes his own crying. "I dissolve my couch with my tears" (Psalms 6:6). "My tears have been my food day and night" (Psalm 42:3).

Usually healing is incomplete without tears. Because tears make others uncomfortable, we may be inclined to use medication to subdue them. Medication can camouflage our emotions and actually interfere with grief-work. Don't be embarrassed or apologize for your tears. Let them flow. People who love you and want to see your healing will not be offended by them. Tears lighten our heaviness for a while.

Another part of this healing process is talking. Usually other people feel they should say wise or witty words to us when we're grieving. I remember Joe Bayly's comments on people who came to be with him after his child had died. One talked to him and tried to say encouraging things. He wished he'd go away. Another came and sat by him in silence. Somehow, it was comforting, and he was sorry to see him go. Our words of comfort often sound glib and flat. Good intentions can't replace good listening.

Talking releases tensions. Rather than magnifying pain, it eases the hurt. Listeners may want to silence the one who's hurting, "Try not to think about that now. You've got to live for the future." The fact is that future living depends on sorting out the past. We can become free of dependence on the past by talking about it, sorting it out, and filing it for a source of future strength instead of an unresolved issue. Talking can bring to the surface feelings that should be faced. Sometimes loneliness surfaces, sometimes anger, guilt, or hostility. All of these need to be resolved. First, they must be faced.

The honesty of children can help us. Mrs. King cared for our brood while I taught classes, shopped, and just escaped. Her retired husband came too, and played catch with the boys, wove tales, and took them on walks. We had planned for her to help us for several days while I took a writing class. Nine days before the course began, Mr. King died unexpectedly during the night. We didn't expect Irene to come the next week, but she insisted that she wanted to. Bob and I explained as simply as we could to our children—ages ten, seven, five, and three—that he had died and that we didn't know whether Mrs. King would want to talk about it or not.

The appointed morning came, and faithful Mrs. King appeared at 7:00 A.M. She stepped in the door, and we exchanged the usual greeting. Pajama-clad little Robby cocked his head when there was a slice of silence. "King's in heaven now?" Dear Mrs. King's eyes filled, and her shoulders relaxed. "Yes," she said with relief. From that moment on there was an openness that put us all at ease.

Insights seldom come from the listener. They are the result of the one who is hurting talking through the issues and the feelings—what he or she can and cannot face at the time.

Grief can make our thinking fuzzy. Realizing that is normal, we need not worry about it. Having a good listener helps us to keep a degree of balance and can keep us from making some wrong decisions. Not just anyone can be our special listener. One of the positive things that comes from our grieving is that we become aware of those friends who can accept us as we are. We come to appreciate those who are looking out for our best interests and are around several months after the crisis. "Rejoice with those who rejoice, and weep with those who weep"

(Romans 12:12). There is great comfort in having a friend who allows us to "feel" and accepts those feelings as we share them.

Hallucinations and dreams are common partners of crisis. Tim's father died unexpectedly when he was ten. His father had promised to build a bird cage with him on Saturday. That accident on Thursday night meant they would never build anything together again. Of course, losing his father was traumatic to Tim. Seeing the unfinished project was a painful reminder. One night Tim dreamed that his father was in his room. His father apologized for not helping him build the bird cage and asked his forgiveness. Somehow this dream comforted Tim. Dad hadn't really intended to let Tim down. That was important to a ten-year-old boy.

We said earlier that we are more susceptible to illness when we are grieving. Try not to neglect your health. It seems like such empty advice, I know.

> Life must go on
> And the dead be forgotten.
> Life must go on
> Though good men die.
> Anne, eat your breakfast;
> Dan, take your medicine.
> Life must go on,
> I forget just why.*

We really may not care about ourselves. But the caring will come back, and additional pain from illness will not drown our grief. If there is optional surgery, postpone it. Let your body do its grief-work before taking on anything else.

Beware of making big decisions during this time. It is not a good time to buy a house, get rid of all your furniture, or remarry. Likely your motivation for doing those things is either to forget the past or replace the person you lost. The impact of the person you lost will never be forgotten. He or she will be integrated into your future. No person can fill another's shoes. Those major decisions should be postponed until more of the grief work is accomplished. You may then choose to remarry, and the

* From COLLECTED POEMS, Harper & Row. Copyright 1921, 1948 by Edna St. Vincent Millay.

foundation will be better. You may find there is comfort in the old furniture when the edge of pain is lessened.

It may help to write down the ways that your life is changing. This is not easy, but it begins a process of thinking about your loss that opens the way for change. One widow found it therapeutic to visit the area where she and her husband had begun their married life. She visited the home where they raised their children. This helped her focus on the good years of their marriage rather than the last months of illness and the hospital experience.

New activities can only begin when you have emotional energy to invest in them. Find new interests. Take classes or begin a new hobby. Discover volunteer projects where you can invest in other people. Return some of the favors that have been shown you. Usually we do not have the strength or the clarity of mind to begin those activities soon after we have begun grieving. Within months, though, we can begin to explore the possibilities.

Steps to Take

1. Realize that grief is a normal reaction following losing someone or something valuable to you.
2. Cry when you feel like it. Your tears are not a sign of weakness or lack of faith. This is direct and immediate therapy for the emotional and physical pain you feel.
3. Talk about your feelings with someone who can listen. Share your plans so that you have a sounding board when making decisions.
4. When you have the emotional energy to invest, discover ways to invest your life in new areas. Beginning a new career or hobby, taking classes, volunteering to help others will help you refocus your dependence on the present and future.

How you can help someone else work through her grief:

1. Let her express the full range of her emotions. Initially this may include denial. Don't support false hopes; however, do not force her to face facts that she may not be able to

face yet. Acceptance often comes slowly. Guilt may be expressed. Even if it is not valid, allow the person to express it. Lazarus's sister Mary expressed anger at Jesus, and He didn't reprove her. These emotions will be worked through more quickly if they are expressed rather than repressed. Repressed emotions usually result in later depression.

2. Be a good listener. You may hear much that is illogical and unrealistic. That does not mean it is not real to the person feeling it! When grief is intense, we attack ourselves. We believe we are responsible for what we had no control over. As a listener, allow those feelings to be expressed whether they are realistic or not. Your verbal denials or logic will probably not be heard. Just listen.

3. Be a sounding-board when it comes to making decisions. Discourage your friend from making major commitments or changes while he or she is grieving. Many newly divorced women make drastic moves which don't work out. One woman moved from Illinois to Texas after her divorce. Her five teenagers could not cope with the drastic change in life-style in addition to losing their father. Within a year they moved back, having suffered financially but especially emotionally from trying to make too many adjustments at once.

4. Stay around. When crisis comes, people flock to old friends—for a week or two. Most grief is more intense after those few weeks are over. The numbness wears off and the adjustments stare coldly and stubbornly in our face. A phone call, a card, a change of scenery, a listening ear as the weeks and months roll by—this is the stuff true friends are made of.

> I cry aloud with my voice to the LORD;
> I make supplication with my voice to the LORD.
> I pour out my complaint before Him;
> I declare my trouble before Him.
> When my spirit was overwhelmed within me,
> Thou didst know my path. . . . I cried out to Thee,
>   O LORD;
> I said, "Thou art my refuge,

My portion in the land of the living.
Give heed to my cry,
For I am brought very low;
Deliver me from my persecutors.
For they are too strong for me."

Psalm 142:1-3a; 5-6

12

Bitterness and Hatred

Bitterness—the sin in good standing. And why not? It can be smoothed out to lie flat under the tablecloth. All the relatives can pull their chairs up around the table and eat right off the top of it. Brother can sit across the table from brother with bitterness rolled out between them. "He got the breaks I should have had. He got the attention that the folks should have shared with me." Excuse after excuse tries to cover it, and most of them appear to be legitimate.

"If they had given me the financial help they gave him—"

"If I'd been the youngest—"

On it goes. Most of the guests are not aware that the roots of bitterness have taken hold. Bitterness, however, is infectious. Don't spouses eventually become entangled? Don't children sense the strain?

Bitterness can fit snugly over the board table at church. "He has more clout, and I work much harder! It's not fair." "There are so few women represented here. Our needs will not be met."

Sibling eyes her sister. Employee eyes her fellow-worker, who is the boss's favorite. We do not have to search in unusual places to find bitterness. A sin in good standing moves in anywhere, regardless of company, organization, or socio-economic level. It coexists with people so well that it is seldom snatched by the corners, rolled up, and thrown into the garbage to be burned.

"See to it that no one comes short of the grace of God; that no root of bitterness springing up causes trouble, and by it many be defiled" (Hebrews 12:15).

Today's common prescription for bitterness (unfortunately even in Christian circles) is to suppress it. Disaster! Suppressed bitterness simply takes the grotesque shape of a mutation. Perhaps the distortion seems less obvious for the moment, but bitterness will surely continue to grow as long as it has a live root.

Its most common shape is hatred. We cannot manage hatred until we have managed bitterness. When we kill bitterness, hatred usually dies of natural causes or goes up in the same smoke.

"How do I keep it from growing?" we ask. Apply a simple biological truth: Dead roots don't grow. We must destroy the roots of bitterness. Before we look at how to kill bitterness, let us look at the seed from which its roots grow.

Visualize a hospital nursery. In neat little rows of cribs tiny little bundles lie and sleep or squirm or cry. Differences emerge already: some are boys, and some are girls. Some are ruddy, with piercing dark eyes and a halo of straight, dark hair. Others have pastel pink scalps, glowing without a trace of hair. Some sleep twenty-four hours and open one eye when they are hungry. Others catnap between fussing and fuming. Feeding time, in their opinion, should be a continuous twenty-four hour process.

Regardless of the differences, each little person is identical in one way. Invisibly tatooed across each little chest is a sign that says, "I Am Important." Each little person as he grows will attempt to prove that sign to be true. Anyone who interferes with the process will be the object of bitterness and perhaps hatred. One person may try to amass wealth to prove himself. Another may try to build a reputation by knowing the right people and dropping the right names. Someone else may want to be a sex symbol or uniquely eye-catching. "Clout" wears different costumes for different people, but the underlying need is the same.

What happens when someone takes a rung out of our ladder to success? We become bitter. Parents become bitter toward their children because their behavior brings humiliation. Their "I Am Important" sign becomes tarnished. A woman becomes bitter toward her brother-in-law because of a failing business in which her husband invested. A girl may sense bitterness toward the man whose love she wants desperately. The bitterness changes to hatred when she sees him with someone else.

How often bitterness is the result of unreturned love. But is it really love, if it must be returned to be valid? Perhaps it is just her ego that needs feeding. A person is often willing to give a semblance of love in order to get something that will feed his or her ego.

How many affairs are an attempt to prove that "I Am Important" sign? "Someone still finds me appealing," the middle-aged-plus person thinks. The rejected youth says, "I've never made it big yet. Nobody's ever wanted me. Maybe in this adventure I'll be somebody." How can any person give himself to another for a no-commitment, no-strings-attached relationship without bitterness resulting?

A little-publicized fact is that affairs are damaging to the self-image. The short-term ego boost becomes the long-term hurt. "He didn't love me enough to marry me." When there is no commitment, there is the hammering reminder that says, "I've been used." The thing that made me feel important now tears at my personhood. Bitterness is unavoidable, though it may be submerged or disguised under an "I didn't care anyway" mask.

Look again at that hospital nursery. Each little infant is wearing another invisible sign. It reads, "I Am Different." Now, God intended each of us to be different, or He wouldn't have created us that way. Differences mean that a team can do lots of things. Watching a good athletic event shows this. Healthy competition results from our differences. But so does bitterness.

What is the solution, then? Here we have a world full of people wanting to feel important by trying to get everyone else's pat on the back. Many efforts fail and result in bitterness. The other person is too busy to care, because he's polishing his own "I Am Important" sign.

Except for the Lord, there is no solution. Three important facts He gives us will help us manage bitterness. First, we realize we are important because: 1) We are created by God. 2) We are loved by God. 3) We are redeemed by Christ. Jesus loved us enough to exchange His life for ours. We are important.

Second, God has committed Himself to supplying our needs. He has not promised us that other people will not let us down or that they will love us to the degree that we need to be loved He has not promised that we will receive recognition in the world or that we will have clout. His promise is simply this: "And my God shall supply all your needs according to His riches in glory in Christ Jesus" (Philippians 4:19).

To expect other people to do what only God can do is to ask for a bushel of bitterness seeds. Then, with each disappointment we experience in relationships, we grab a handful and throw them to the ground. With each fresh hurt we pour fertilizer on our sprouting bitterness seeds. "See what he could have done for me?" "See how she ignores me?" "See the verbal dart he just threw?" "See the love that brother stole that was rightfully mine?" "See the money squandered?" "See? See? See?" The bitterness bush thrives and becomes a tree of hatred that reproduces a forest. The forest of hatred envelopes us and keeps the sunshine out. The person wandering in it must cut and chop to take a step forward. Bitterness is indeed a harsh taskmaster.

Why is it especially easy to become bitter toward relatives? My "Titus woman," Polly Hahn, taught me some valuable lessons related to this. "We expect more from our relatives than we do from our closest friends," she explained. I could see that in my own life. Though some of my relatives hardly know me, I expect their sympathy and support. When a new individual marries into the family, I expect her to know my history and my unique (translated "weird" by my daughter) traits.

We often assume a closeness in our relationships that we don't take time to build. We assume there should be understanding, though we may not communicate well. No wonder bitterness often finds good growing conditions in families.

We must internalize the fact that God is the ultimate source of all our needs.

"For my father and my mother have forsaken me, but the LORD will take me up" (Psalm 27:10).

"For your husband is your Maker, whose name is the LORD of hosts" (Isaiah 54:5).

" 'For the mountains may be removed and the hills may shake, but My lovingkindness will not be removed from you, and My covenant of peace will not be shaken,' says the LORD who has compassion on you" (Isaiah 54:10).

"Now the God of peace, who brought up from the dead the great Shepherd of the sheep through the blood of the eternal covenant, even Jesus our Lord, equip you in every good thing to do His will . . ." (Hebrews 13:20-21a).

God is the only reliable source. Only He has enough of everything.

You shout, "I see! I see! So God supplies all of our needs. But it's too late. What do I do with my hatred? What do I do with my bitterness?"

Forgive. This simple seven-letter word holds the key to every successful relationship. Marriages, business partnerships, friendships, and one's emotional survival when completely alone are all determined by those seven letters. We can't live with ourselves unless we have learned to forgive.

Don't wait for the person who let you down to come to ask for forgiveness; it will probably never happen. The greatest hurt I ever experienced was inflicted by one who will never know the heartache that was caused.

Can I afford to spend my lifetime with bitterness and hatred as my taskmaster? I have chosen not to! By an act of my own will (and the Lord's enabling) I have determined I will be free of hatred. I will be free of bitterness. I will forgive. Forgiveness means I agree to bear the pain, absorb the loss, accommodate the knife in my back or in my heart. In my humanness this is impossible. I think every person has a space marked "unforgivable."

The slave in Matthew 25:28 had a space marked "unforgivable." It was one third of his annual salary that was uncollectable. Proportions of the space vary, but they are all pain-filled and provide topsoil for bitterness.

"Here, Lord. I roll the pain onto Your shoulders. I cannot bear it alone. Lord, the failure and disappointment I roll onto You. Your prophets said that the government will be upon Your shoulders (Isaiah 9:6). The government of my life I commit to You. I have something more to bring to You, Lord; You've asked for it all. Here's my hurt. The bitterness is gone, but the hurt remains. I must be free of it, too! I need the warmth of Your purifying fire."

How warm is the sunshine when the forest of hatred has been burned. Isaiah 61:3 becomes a reality, as beauty replaces ashes; the oil of gladness replaces mourning; and a garment of praise replaces the spirit of despair.

Bitterness changes the most beautiful features to ugliness. The radiating glow of forgiveness creates a beauty that coaxes a smile from the pedestrian hurrying by. Forgiveness changes the smothering, suffocating air in a room full of relatives. God knows that one of our most important needs is to forgive. He intends to supply it, but He cannot until we admit that it is a need and ask for Him to do it. I found that He filled my "unforgivable" space with three commodities that hadn't been there before: compassion, love, and understanding.

I began to feel pity for the one who had hurt me. Forgiveness took my focus from myself to him and allowed me to see the kind of life that had led to that behavior. The love was not something I had manufactured, but something I had to ask God for—I still do. Understanding was the result of beginning to see the world through the other person's eyes. I could give him room to be human and imperfect, because his hurt would no longer control my life.

A classic case of bitterness in the Bible is the story of the prodigal son. Do you remember the older brother? When his father celebrated his younger brother's return, this man sulked.

> Look! For so many years I have been serving you, and I have never neglected a command of yours; and yet you have never given me a kid, that I might be merry with my friends; but when this son of yours came, who has devoured your wealth with harlots, you killed the fattened calf for him. [Luke 15:29-30]

"You should be polishing my 'I Am Important' sign. I've earned it," he says.

And his father answered, "Everything I have is yours."

Jesus told this parable to illustrate the problem the Pharisees had. They were bitter. Jesus' spiritual power was obvious. Common people like the disciples were learning from Him. Broken people were being healed, and the Pharisees were sulking. "We are the great spiritual leaders, aren't we? We should be getting the attention. Great crowds should be flocking around our robes for blessing."

Greater dissension was yet to rear its ugly head when the Gentiles ("dogs" they were called) received God's blessing; some of the Hebrew Christians resented their freedom. The Lord's answer to their bitterness was the same as it is for us: God's riches are great enough to go around. No one will be left out, unless he is hiding in the forest of bitterness. God's supply is sufficient.

Remember Jonah? Picture him sitting outside of Nineveh. He had proclaimed that the city would be destroyed for its wickedness. Jonah was a prophet who saw results. The people repented, fasted, and covered themselves with ashes, but most of all, they turned from their evil ways! And Jonah sulked!

Why? Maybe it would have glorified Jonah if God had rained down fire as He did on Sodom and Gomorrah. The world would have said, "Now there goes a man of power." But God is forgiving. Righteous living doesn't attract the attention that judgment of sin does, but it pleases God more. The people of Nineveh were glorifying God, not Jonah. And Jonah was sulking.

Look at Jonah 4:5-9. As I read through those verses, repeatedly I see the phrase "God provided." God provided a vine. God provided a worm. God provided a scorching east wind. Was God out to get Jonah? Of course not. He was providing for Jonah's need. And Jonah's great need at that moment was to learn more about the heart of God. God was richly supplying Jonah's need, though much of it didn't please Jonah much.

Our opportunity to be bitter is usually our opportunity to see more of God's power, His great desire to satisfy us, and His openness to reveal Himself to us.

Steps to Take

1. What makes you feel important?
2. Why should you feel important?
3. Are you bitter? Toward whom do you feel bitter and why?
4. What changes would result in your feelings and behavior if you were no longer bitter?
5. Are you willing to absorb the loss and pain by forgiving?

6. Ask God to give you love for the other person involved.
7. Ask God to show you other "unforgivable" spaces you might have.

> Do return, O LORD; how long will it be?
> And be sorry for Thy servants.
> O satisfy us in the morning with Thy loving kindness,
> That we may sing for joy and be glad all our days.
> Make us glad according to the days Thou hast
>   afflicted us,
> And the years we have seen evil.
> Let Thy work appear to Thy servants,
> And Thy majesty to their children.
> And let the favor of the LORD our God be upon us;
> And do confirm for us the work of our hands;
> Yes, confirm the work of our hands.

Psalm 90:13-17

13

Guilt

Guilt—tenacious, gnawing—the emotion we'd probably like to sweep under the rug. But as much as we dislike it, guilt is a valuable emotion.

"Not this feeling I'm struggling with," you say. "My father expected me to be a financial success. I never achieved what he expected of me while he was alive. I'll never be free from the guilt of letting him down. What's positive about that?"

There are two kinds of guilt: real guilt and false guilt. Real guilt (or "value guilt," as Paul Tournier, a Christian physician from Switzerland, calls it) is constructive, because it makes us feel uncomfortable over things we've done wrong or wrong attitudes we've had. This guilt brings us to an attitude of repentance. Often the Holy Spirit uses this feeling in our lives to bring us to accepting Jesus Christ as our Savior. Second Corinthians 7:10 elaborates on this: "For the sorrow that is according to the will of God produces a repentance without regret, leading to salvation; but the sorrow of the world produces death." Real guilt is based on violating God's instruction and the truths of His Word.

False guilt is the emotion we feel when we violate some person's expectation of us—when that expectation is not based on God's expectation. Much false guilt stems from childhood training.

A little girl may be taught that sex is bad or dirty. Her parents teach her this, hoping it will keep her "pure" until she marries. The result is that when she marries, she cannot enjoy the physical relationship with her husband. She feels false guilt. Her husband believes his wife is frigid. In a marriage like this intercourse occurs seldom—just when they want children. The husband is tempted to satisfy his need outside the marriage relationship. If he does this, he experiences real guilt, because he knows he's violating God's moral standard.

Real Guilt

The solution to guilt begins with determining whether it is real or false. Do you feel guilty because you have cheated someone—you took more than she intended to give you? Are you bitter or jealous? Did you take someone's sense of worth or take advantage of her openness? Are you nursing a grudge? If so, then your guilt is real, because those things violate Scripture. The solution for real guilt is simpler than the solution for false guilt. It is this:

1. Apologize to the people or person you have wronged, if they are aware of the problem.
2. Ask for forgiveness from the individual and from God.
3. Make restitution when possible. Zacchaeus returned fourfold what he had "stolen" from the taxpayers (see Luke 19:8).
4. Go on from there (Philippians 3:13-14: "forgetting what lies behind and reaching forward to what lies ahead, I press on").

You may be looking at step 1 and thinking, "But shouldn't we always get it all out into the open?"

We hear that even from popular Bible teachers today: "Whether or not the other person is aware of your hostility or unfaithfulness or envy or hatred, confess it to him/her. Lay it all out on the table. You'll feel so much closer after it's all over." That is indeed one possibility, but a slim one.

There are other possibilities. The person who is unaware of your ill-feeling, upon learning of it, may first be surprised and then hurt. If he (or she) is spiritually mature, forgiveness will follow eventually. However, many Christians are not mature. It may be a long time before they can forgive, and they may never be able to forget.

In the meantime, you've put a stumbling block in that person's path. Now the other person is tempted to respond to you with dislike, distrust, or anger—to name a few feelings. If the other person involved is not even aware of your problem, is it not better simply to ask *God's* forgiveness, and go on from there?

Early one morning my phone rang. A friend needed help. She felt drawn to another man. As a mutual friend, her husband knew him well. She sensed that the attraction was a two-way street. What should she do?

After hearing a radio program, she concluded that she should sit down with her husband and confess her sin to him.

"And what would he do?" I asked.

"Oh! He'd be furious! He'd fuss and fume and no telling what else. It would be weeks or maybe months before he could settle down and our relationship return to normal."

In our soap opera generation, this sounds like a great way to deal with the problem. Then to make sure the "air was clear" and everything was "out in the open," she could call the man she was attracted to. She could arrange to meet him alone so that she could confess her sin. Maybe it would set an example for him, right? Highly unlikely! Compromising circumstances can be our undoing. (When Jonah wanted to run away, he just happened to find a ship that just happened to have room for him so that he could run away from God.)

The meeting could become an opportunity for the attraction to grow. Then, if their secret meeting should accidently become public knowledge and his mate find out, they would face all sorts of struggles; there would be the opportunity for all four of them to be closer because of all they'd been through together!

We have enough struggles and battles to fight without maximizing the effects of sin. Would it not glorify God more for this girl to confess her sin to God alone?

Having asked His forgiveness, we must then accept it. Feeling worthy of His forgiveness is irrelevant. First John 1:9 says, "If we confess our sins, He is faithful and righteous to forgive us our sins and to cleanse us from all unrighteousness." Fact. We simply accept it. In this case, there was no restitution to be made.

For my friend the fourth step in managing real guilt will be the hardest. "Go on from there." Those are such simple words, but how do we live them? The "how to" will be as varied as the unique individuals involved. My friend will probably find it necessary to do much additional praying after that prayer for forgiveness.

Lord, it gave my ego a boost to see that I would catch his eye, You know I haven't felt so positive about myself lately. You want me to be satisfied. Assure me again of how much You love me, how much You like me, how special I am to You.

Maybe that's not the problem at all. Perhaps this prayer ought to follow:

Lord, I've been sloppy in my marriage commitment. The past that you've forgiven keeps interfering with today. I've let down on my commitment of mental faithfulness to my husband. With Your help I want to invest more of myself, more of my time, more of my love in our marriage.

Perhaps these couples can continue their friendship. Perhaps not. If the temptation is too strong, the way of escape (1 Corinthians 10:13) may be no more meetings and communication. It would be better to put the friendship on the expendable list, rather than the marriage.

Forgiving real guilt is God's specialty. Since violating His desires is what causes real guilt, it is logical that we go to Him for the solution. We may attempt other solutions, such as throwing our guilt in a back room of our mind and pretending it's not there. Or we may blame our behavior on someone else, claiming that we were helplessly swept along into the mess. But those detours are usually not workable—even on a short-term basis, not to speak of the long haul.

There is a fifth child who lives at our house called "Nobody." I was cleaning under the basement stairs on my once-every-two-years cleaning plan. On the dark cement in a corner I found moldy apple cores, black, brittle banana peels, and peach seeds. It looked like someone had been operating a fruit stand or collecting compost to fertilize a garden. I called our offspring to give accounts of themselves. By the time the lineup had all had his/her turn to reply, the unanimous decision was that "Nobody" had done it. "Great," I wanted to scream, "Will 'Nobody' please crawl back there and clean it up?" Within a few days I discovered that "Nobody" also liked to eat in the attic. I stumbled across assorted containers with remains of spaghettios and chocolate pudding.

"Nobody" breaks windows, eats the frosting off cakes before company comes, leaves gallon boxes of ice cream on the kitchen counter before we leave the house for three hours, and delights in parking bicycles behind the car. "Nobody" puts crayons in the clothes dryer and is not even tax-deductible!

Somehow even our little children can't let "Nobody" bear all that guilt forever. Eventually a little form appears in our darkened doorway at night or perhaps comes into the laundry room "just to see if I'm doing the wash." Sometimes he wants to ride alone with Daddy to the hardware store. By the time they return, "Nobody" is free from another misdemeanor. Spiritual infants may blame someone else, but there will be no maturing until there is confession and forgiveness. A feeling of freedom energizes us when we are forgiven.

Unfortunately, that feeling is temporary. The battle is won, and God has forgiven. But the war rages on. God has forgotten, but I keep remembering. Restitution has been made, but I mark the account. "Miriam, you'll never finish paying for this one." Paul said he forgot the past, with all of his sin and rebellion. I'm not Paul, but what worked for him is helping me. Before he forgot the past, he put it in perspective.

One lesson Paul learned was that God wasn't stumped by anyone's past. King Solomon's parents were David and Bathsheba. Wouldn't Abigail have been a better mother? Solomon's Temple was built on the ground where David had offered sacrifices for numbering the people. Wasn't there any piece of nearby real estate that wasn't so bloodsoaked?

We cannot understand all of God's choices. He seems to pass up some prime candidates—which means I'm still in the running. "This is how we shall know that we are children of the truth and can reassure ourselves in the sight of God, even if our own conscience makes us feel guilty. For God is greater than our conscience, and he knows everything" (1 John 3:19-20, Phillips).

God is able to retrain my conscience. He knows what kind of material He can use for His glory. I mistakenly think He is looking for material marked "marketable," "acceptable after public scrutiny," or "this product has never been opened." Instead, He gathers materials marked "overstock," "needs rewiring," and "overhaul necessary." We think we are picked because we've hidden our weak spots, but the truth is, God chooses us in spite of them. "He knows everything."

It's easier to forget the past when I crowd past sins out with these facts. Let's review the solution for real guilt.

Steps to Take

1. Apologize to the people or person you have wronged, if they are aware of the problem.
2. Ask for forgiveness from the individual and from God.
3. Make restitution when possible.
4. Live with the freedom of forgiveness. Why remember what God has chosen to forget?

> Be gracious to me, O God, according to Thy
>   lovingkindness;
> According to the greatness of Thy compassion blot out
>   my transgressions.
> Wash me thoroughly from my iniquity,
> And cleanse me from my sin.
> For I know my transgressions,
> And my sin is ever before me.
> Against Thee, Thee only, I have sinned,
> And done what is evil in Thy sight. . . .
> Purify me with hyssop, and I shall be clean;
> Wash me, and I shall be whiter than snow. . . .
> Create in me a clean heart, O God,
> And renew a steadfast spirit within me. . . .
> Restore to me the joy of Thy salvation,
> And sustain me with a willing spirit.
>
> Psalm 51:1-4a, 7, 10, 12

False Guilt

What do we do with false guilt? We've already said that false guilt usually results from our failure to measure up to some person's expectation of us. Many times we do not acknowledge false guilt for what it is. It feels like real guilt. We ask for God's forgiveness, but we continue to experience guilt feelings. We don't know where to turn.

Our best offense against guilt is God's Word. Unfortunately, many bodies of believers have added to His Word and laid heavy burdens on people. Groups and individuals impose these "extras" as their super-spiritual yardsticks, with which they measure others, determining who will be "in" and who will be "out." These "extras" make non-Christians want to avoid the "in" group like the plague. Of course, this makes evangelism very difficult.

Usually those "in" groups are too busy retyping their "do's and don'ts" lists to recall Matthew 28:19: "Go therefore and make disciples of all the nations, baptizing them in the name of the Father and the Son and the Holy Spirit." Matthew 28:20 tells us what to do after we have brought these new disciples to Jesus—"and teaching them to observe all that I commanded you." Simple instructions: If our Lord has not commanded it, by no means should we.

Jesus rebuked the religious leaders of his time: "Woe to you lawyers as well! For you weigh men down with burdens hard to bear, while you yourselves will not even touch the burdens with one of your fingers" (Luke 11:46).

How many little children grow up in a "church" setting, only to reject Christ? What happened? Children often get a good look at those extra burdens, instead of at Jesus. Their response is, "No." The "extras" only hinder the impact and appeal of the gospel.

How many people are trying to conform to what they think God expects of them? Much false guilt would be pushed aside if we searched the Scriptures to find His instructions. If you are suffering with this kind of false guilt, study especially the book of Galatians. Paul pointed the Galatians to God's love and grace. It's available for us. Bruce Narramore summarized this in *Freedom from Guilt*: "The law says, 'perform so you will be accepted.' Grace says, 'you're accepted, now you can perform.' "*

False guilt results from false teachers in the body of believers. But there is a greater source of false guilt: childhood training.

* Bruce Narramore, *Freedom from Guilt* (Irvine, Calif.: Harvest House, 1976).

First I should say, dear parent, I am not out to get you, and I know your job is not an easy one. But we need to be careful that we do not produce false guilt in our children.

What role does the parent play in producing false guilt?

Minirth and Meier summarize it by saying that overly strict parents can cause a child to develop a low self-concept. The child assumes that his parents' view of him is correct, so he blames himself for his imperfections. As he becomes a teenager or adult, his anger toward himself may lead to clinical depression.

The overly-strict parent that Minirth and Meier describes seldom (or sometimes never) compliments his child. If he does, he quickly follows his compliment with an admonition to do better or a reminder of some other little mistake. The child is never allowed to stand and smile, completely smothered with acceptance. A touch of pain is always administered with the pleasure.

The overly strict parent also produces false guilt in a child by ignoring him. Occasionally you can tell a child anything; you might tell him that you love him and that he's important to you. But never interact with your child; never develop a person-to-person relationship with him; and never ask him questions about himself or what he's doing. Most of all, never ask him how he feels about anybody or anything. Your child will grow up believing he's a nonentity. You may see no visible or conscious evidence of this until the child is an adult, but the whole foundation will have been laid.

The child who cannot relate to his parent believes there must be something wrong with him, since he can't get his father's or mother's attention. This child may strive all of his life to meet his parents' expectations of him. If he doesn't know what pleases them, he will make up goals that he believes will get their attention. Every unreached goal will add to his burden of false guilt. It's not enough for a child to hear that he is loved, although that is a good beginning. The love must be lived so that he can see and feel it.

Dr. James Dobson says that a great portion of our adult effort is invested in the quest for that which was unreachable in childhood. As children we desperately need our parents' approval. We constantly probe to discover what would please them. Their whim or desire becomes our life ambition, the direction for our profession, the key to our emotional wholeness. Whether their expectations are reasonable, godly, or reachable is irrelevant to a child's mind.

There's at least one more common producer of guilt. Misdirected or pent-up anger produces both real and false guilt. When we refuse to acknowledge that we are angry, we feel guilty. We cannot release denied anger. It grinds and tears and makes us think of what we'd like to do to the person who is its object. Perhaps we are too "mature" to do something horrible; we hope someone else (or fate) will. All of our unrealized, misdirected, or denied anger makes us feel guilty.

Guilt caused by pent-up anger is often combined with guilt carried over from childhood. If we feel we have never gained our parents' approval, we become angry at them. Ironically, we never label it as anger. In fact, we may never realize how much of our behavior is twisted by this unhappy combination of guilt. Our anger may surface when aging parents become demanding. Perhaps a stroke causes a parent to require more physical care. Perhaps a change in living conditions results in their dialing our number more often to satisfy their needs. Submerged anger is likely to be pushed to the surface under the strain.

Look at this time as an opportunity to manage false guilt. You are likely to experience freedom and satisfaction you never could have otherwise, had you not been faced with this conflict. James says, "When all kinds of trials and temptations crowd into your lives, my brothers, don't resent them as intruders, but welcome them as friends" (James 1:2, Phillips)!

The Other Generation Gap, by Cohen and Gans, may be especially helpful if you are grappling with the conflict of aging parents.

How can we manage false guilt?

1. We acknowledge it for what it is: false guilt. We mark it an unwelcome intruder which we will not allow to manage us.

2. We forgive the source of false guilt. Forgiving the source of false guilt may be a one-time act of forgiveness. In a few cases it is a step easily taken. However, for most of us it is

one of our greatest spiritual battles. It often must continue for years or perhaps a lifetime. Sometimes hurt surfaces long after we have forgiven what was caused by false teachers or unloving parents. We must forgive again and again.

What causes us to keep remembering the hurt? False guilt is produced over months, if not years. Attitudes and actions are saturated by these expectations. If all the resulting hurt were to surface at once when we were willing to forgive, it would be overwhelming. Isaiah 42:3 gently reassures us, "A bruised reed He will not break, and a dimly burning wick He will not extinguish." God graciously allows us to remember only what we can forgive at the time. In later housecleanings He will reveal more. But His grace and His knowledge of the precious person He created in us move His hands to only give us what we can accept at each moment.

3. We go on from there. How? With leaps and bounds and shouts of joy. How freeing to be unbound from false guilt! How energizing to be able to look at what we would like to do with our hours and abilities with God's blessing. False guilt has yoked us long enough to some person or group's expectation. Now we can move on ahead with the Lord. Our only yoke is to Him, and it is easy and light (see Matthew 11:30).

This is how we feel when the light goes on; we recognize our false guilt and anger for what it is. At this point we need to be cautious. Remember, emotions are habit-forming. Our mind has grasped the solution, but our emotions need to be retrained. Circumstances will trigger that old anger and guilt. A parent's word or even expression may stir that false guilt in us. Suddenly, we're ready to retreat to our old feelings of inadequacy and "if only" attitude. That false guilt is unjustified, so we review the facts in our mind and select an appropriate new reaction to the old barb. Then we repeat it until it has squeezed out our old feeling of false guilt.

Steps to Take

1. Habitually read the Bible. No other activity will spotlight and unmask false guilt.

2. Forgive the source of false guilt.
3. Identify the barbs (people, places, feelings, items) that trigger false guilt in you.
4. Decide on an appropriate God-honoring reaction to that barb.
5. Practice the reaction until it replaces false guilt.

Remember my affliction and my wandering, the wormwood and bitterness.
Surely my soul remembers
And is bowed down within me.
This I recall to my mind,
Therefore I have hope.
The LORD's lovingkindnesses indeed never cease,
For His compassions never fail,
They are new every morning;
Great is Thy faithfulness.
"The LORD is my portion," says my soul,
"Therefore I have hope in Him."

Lamentations 3:19-24

14

Breaking Emotional Habits

We have referred to emotions as the tentacles of an octopus. Do you want to manage them or be chased by them? We have referred to them as a web. Do you want to be the spider or the fly? Knowledge of the facts on which emotions are based is essential to their healthy expression. But knowing the facts is not enough.

Emotions are similar to actions in that they are habit-forming. Just as we form habits of behavior, we form emotional habits. Habits aren't always bad. You get up in the morning. You don't consciously think, "I'll put one foot on the floor. Now I'll put the other foot beside it. I'll put one in front of the other until I reach the toothpaste." Fortunately, by repeating actions, they become habits and then we don't have to labor through conscious struggles to accomplish every task. Habits facilitate efficient living. Habits free us to expand, to grow.

Some habits aren't helpful. We can develop the habit of overeating. I find it easy to drink more coffee than I should. A sign by my coffee pot reads, "I'm not nervous, just incredibly alert!" I needn't say that habits are hard to break; you already know that. Erwin Lutzer has written an excellent book on breaking habits. It's entitled *How to Say No to a Stubborn Habit.** Maybe this chapter could be called "How To Say 'No' to a Stubborn Emotional Habit."

We know that our emotions respond to actions and events in our lives. As these actions and events draw the same emotional

---

* Erwin Lutzer, *How to Say No to a Stubborn Habit* (Wheaton, Ill.: Victor, 1979).

response from us, we form a habit. Many of these emotional habits are formed in childhood and become firmly established during adulthood. But we can choose either to live with them or to change them. We cannot change them until we change our minds about the facts involved. After we've changed our minds, we have to retrain our emotions. Changing bad emotional habits is usually a lengthy process.

Evelyn was a bitter woman. She had developed the habit of bitterness. She expected that everyone was out to do her in. She believed that her relatives didn't treat her right. She expected her car repairman to do less than she asked of him. She expected her financial advisors to try to trick her. Her emotional life was dominated by bitterness. Practically every event in her life was affected by that habit. Will her bitterness disappear when she learns God loves her? Will she automatically believe that God will supply her needs? Will forgiving those who have mistreated her in the past be a once-and-for-all victory over bitterness? It is possible, but not probable. God sometimes works instantly. He can; He's able. But usually He doesn't.

Evelyn's habit was formed over a long period; the change will take time. Her work begins with internalizing the foundational truths in the chapter on bitterness. Then she must tackle a long-term assignment. When she responds to an event with the beginnings of bitterness, she must arrest that feeling. "There goes my 'skepticism' buzzer. I'm wondering how that person is going to try to take advantage of me. Jesus didn't treat me like that. I'm going to expect the best of that person. I'm going to accept that person without looking for any barbs."

Next, she must edit that feeling. "I'm throwing this bitterness out. It hasn't served me well. It's made me a crab and an old Scrooge, and there are better ways to spend my emotions."

Emotions do not remain in neutral or function well with a void. Replace that bad habit with a good one. In the case of bitterness, we can choose to think of our worth to God. The feeling of completeness that accompanies this crowds out bitterness.

Breaking emotional habits involves the people around us. They have learned to live with us as we are. A change on our part requires a change in them. Though they may suffer from our bad emotional habits, at least they know what to expect from us!

We need to be aware of this so we don't expect support from others that perhaps they cannot give. Change requires that we keep our future goal before us. We realize that the process of change will be painful but worth the struggle.

Have you ever gone on a diet? When were you successful? What brought success? What brought failure? Pardon me for picking such a sensitive subject for us women. But many of the principles for a successful diet parallel those of breaking bad emotional habits. Fasting for two days doesn't bring permanent results like controlled modified eating habits do. If we consistently catch emotional habits that we wish to change over a period of time and apply biblical truths to them, we will see change.

What happens when you've been "good" all week, and then you win the "Pig for a Day" trophy? You can give up and eat your way through another week. Or you can say, "I won't repeat tomorrow what I did today. Six days were successful, and I'll use those as my guide rather than the 'Pig' day."

This principle applies to our emotions as well. If I've been working to break the habit of anger, likely failure will interrupt my success. How do I respond? I can say to myself, "I didn't see that coming. Anger snagged me first. What triggered it? How can I be better prepared next time?" In some of my own struggles, I have found patterns that trigger bad emotional habits. I am learning to identify these. As I see the signs coming, I can prepare to respond in a new way rather than with the old habit.

I struggle with feelings of inferiority. I have had a habit of looking in the mirror and seeing a woman who is dumb and ugly. Then I feel worthless. God doesn't approve of this. Since I am His daughter, it is a sin to devalue one who is so precious to Him. This feeling breeds bitterness (Whom can I blame?). It also breeds anxiety (How can I measure up? How can I be a somebody?).

I have discovered that part of the solution to my bad emotional habit is to spend some time alone. I can't thoroughly explain why this is so therapeutic to me. Perhaps it is because being around small children is a drain. (I love them, but they tax my emotional storehouse.) Perhaps it is because some of the happiest moments of my childhood were spent roaming the hills of southern Indiana alone. Perhaps it is because God has so often comforted and assured me so completely when I was alone.

Though I don't understand why, I know it is true. I know that my emotions are restored by time spent alone. Jesus needed those times, too, so I'm not ashamed to admit my need for solitude.

What do I do with this knowledge? I must plan for feasible, appropriate ways to be alone. I can occasionally bike to a nearby forest preserve for some moments of solitude. Sometimes I can even arrange a day or two away. Perhaps as I grow stronger this will not be necessary. But for now, it is a part of breaking an emotional habit that has often been a strangling tentacle in my life.

What triggers some of your bad emotional habits? Does listening to music with twisted messages cause feelings of infatuation or lust that crowd out love as defined by God? What steps can you take to change those habits? Where are you going and with whom? Are your companions part of the problem or the solution? We can find "friends" who feed our bad habits. Remember Amnon and Jonadab?

When we make the decision to break an bad emotional habit, we may find our relationships changing. Some friendships will become less important. Some people will not seek out our company as they have in the past. The sifting will bring changes, and a new and better balance will establish itself.

What part do our consciences play in emotional habits? A lot! As Dr. James Dobson points out in *Emotions—Can You Trust Them?* our consciences are largely a gift from our parents.* Since our parents are fallible, sometimes they train our consciences to direct us in ways that coincide with God's principles, but not always. Our consciences remind us of what brought the approval or disapproval of our parents. What if your conscience has learned principles that are not biblical? It is possible to redirect our consciences. "How much more will the blood of Christ, who through the eternal Spirit offered himself without blemish to God, cleanse your conscience from dead works to serve the living God?" (Hebrews 9:14).

Our consciences are redirected, as the Holy Spirit takes God's Word and applies it to our thoughts and feelings. Suppose my conscience says, "Miriam, the bionic Christian supermom, never

---

* James Dobson, *Emotions: Can You Trust Them?* (Ventura, Calif.: Regal, 1980).

leaves her children for a moment. She hovers over them, suffocates them, and mothers them until she is an exhausted dishrag." This kind of message from my conscience needs to be redirected— for the children's sake as well as my own.

I read in Titus 2:4 that I am to love (*phileo*) my children. I am to love them with brotherly love; I am to like them as friends. This instruction from God's Word redirects my conscience. I leave them for short periods of time. I don't wallow in guilt. They learn that Mama will come home refreshed with more patience and maybe some new experiences to share with them. I know that important steps toward independence will take place during my absence. Precious moments will be treasured between sons and father, daughter and father that would not happen if I were there.

It is vital that we redirect our conscience through the Word rather than to slavishly do what our culture approves. Our culture approves of abortion, mothers deserting children, and mothers disregarding their children's need for a father. A conscience so trained will hardly direct us to serve the living God!

As we work toward breaking bad emotional habits, we must keep reading the Bible. The Holy Spirit uses this avenue to redirect our consciences, if they are not already molded by biblical principles. As our consciences are molded, they can help us, warn us, and encourage us in our growth.

We said earlier that some principles of breaking emotional habits are similar to those used in successful dieting. In our area there is a weight control organization that stresses answering to others for what you eat. The group becomes the authority figure that can either clap if you have lost a few pounds or tell you to go home and stick more closely to the diet. It becomes important to the members to conform to the image of the authority. I find this interesting in our independent age. The same principle is effective in Alcoholics Anonymous. Let's investigate what authority has to do with our emotions.

Our self-concept is derived from the one to whom we feel submission. If your employer is a big name, you state where you work with pride. If you take your orders from a company of ill-repute, you don't sense the worth you might. This applies to school districts, hospitals, banking firms, and most sources of employment.

Our first experience of being in submission to another person occurs with our parents. From them we receive our relative self-concept. This is relative because it depends on many factors. Did they want another redheaded boy? Were their financial burdens foremost in their lives at the time? Did they believe that children are a heritage from the Lord? These changeable factors determine how they treated you. A child has a sense of being owned by his parents, and he derives his sense of worth from how his parents demonstrate his importance to them. If parents are indifferent to their child, that child sees himself as worthless. If parents love their child and effectively communicate this love, the child sees himself as a person of worth.

When we accept God's authority in our lives, our human reaction is to assume that His role will be like our parents'. We assume that His authority will follow the pattern our parents set. If they were indifferent, we assume that God is indifferent. We gained no sense of worth from our parents, and we retain the same emotional habits as adults.

In this case, we discover that we have a bad emotional habit to break. We can choose to remain stagnant Christians and retain the old habit. Perhaps you're living with an indifferent authority figure, and you've learned to exist with your tangled emotions. I believe if we consistently read the Bible, we cannot retain this image of an indifferent God. The image of an authority figure who gives us no sense of worth cannot cohabit with a woman who is living by the Word of God. This principle may trigger understanding of some of your emotional habits. With a handle to understanding these habits, it is easier to consistently snag these emotions and edit them.

One of the most common emotional bad habits for a woman is to devalue herself. Often the source of this is an indifferent father. The woman who has had this experience usually believes her husband is indifferent. She will even try to force him into her father's mold, though he loves her and wants to demonstrate this love. Why? Because for eighteen, or twenty, or twenty-two years she has learned to live with this kind of masculine image. She has learned how to live with this kind of authority.

To have a man treat her as a person of worth does not fit in with her emotional habit of devaluing herself. She expects her husband to have ulterior motives for giving her attention. She seeks continual proof that she is first in his life. She is threatened by his job, especially if it is a good one. If it is a demanding one, she is jealous. She makes impossible demands of him, in order to "prove" that he really doesn't love her.

This woman has to replace this twisted lack of self-worth with God's statement of her absolute worth. "If God is for us, who is against us? He who did not spare His own Son, but delivered Him up for us all, how will He not also with him freely give us all things? . . . Who is the one who condemns? . . . We overwhelmingly conquer through Him who loved us" (Romans 8:31-32, 34, 37).

In our country of comfort, we may think that the problems Paul mentions in Romans 8 are not related to us. As I studied the definitions in *Vine's Expository Dictionary*, I identified with many of them. Some of them we feel; more we fear. Some of the trials are emotional, while others are physical. Famine means lack of food or money. Danger can be threats to our lives or whatever excites anguish. Nakedness means lack of clothes or humiliation. Trouble means catastrophe and disasters or anything that makes a person miserable. Hardship is defined as tight, narrow places—straight and hemmed in on every side, with no possibility of escaping. Persecution is hurt deliberately inflicted (sometimes because we are a Christians) with the intent of destroying. Through every tragedy God always has one objective. He intends to bring us to a stark confrontation of His love. Nothing can come between us and the covering of His love.

I have a friend who spent time in a German concentration camp. She was forced to walk naked with other female prisoners before the prison guards. She cringes as she relives the feelings. But she says she identified with Christ's humiliation on the cross more through that experience than any other. Corrie Ten Boom had the same experience. I don't know Corrie Ten Boom, but I have seen in my friend's life emotional healing through knowing God loves her. She knows God has redeemed her and will some day change her scarred body. It is precious to Him.

"But," you say, "I've *earned* the right to fall apart. Look at all this trouble in my life. I've earned the right to be an emotional basket case."

Yes, perhaps you have, my friend. So have I. But we have a better option. When I believe I have earned the right to fall apart, I snag that feeling and edit it. This is my opportunity to face God as I never have before. May I personalize James 1:2?

> My [sister], whenever you have to face trials of many kinds, count [yourself] supremely happy, in the knowledge that such testing of your faith breeds fortitude, and if you give fortitude full play you will go on to complete a balanced character that will fall short in nothing. [NEB*]

When I was a little girl, Mama would make caramel frosting by cooking all kinds of delicious ingredients in a saucepan. She would set that saucepan in the kitchen window to cool. As soon as it was cool enough to tolerate, I would sneak by and swipe as many fingerfuls as I possibly could before getting caught.

One day, to my surprised delight, I saw the saucepan in the window, with its warm, butter-brown contents. I hadn't known Mama was making caramel that day. In went my fingers for a heavenly mouthful. Arsenic couldn't have tasted worse! Mama's response to my choking and sputtering was that she was making GLUE!

We have lots of emotional freedom as women today. We are encouraged to "tell it like it is." We are encouraged to face our true feelings. We are encouraged to "take our masks off." We are encouraged to give our emotions free rein, and "let it all hang out." Some good may result. But we can eat lots of glue, too. Twisted emotions can be uncovered that actually caused less pain when they were submerged. Actions we used to fake were socially acceptable, and what we may really want to do now is not. Doesn't sound like caramel frosting, does it? Freeing our emotions can become a real pit of glue.

A new battle gives us the opportunity for a new victory. Uncovered emotions need not expose us to self-defeating, destructive activity. Instead, we can be free to become more energized Christian women than ever before. Straightening out our tangled emotions need not threaten those around us or throw precious relationships up for grabs. New emotional habits can enable us to be stronger friends, more loving wives, and better

* *The New English Bible.*

mothers. Our renewed, refilled emotional tanks can be sources of vibrant living that are salt to a pretty flat-tasting world.

Our bodies can be better tuned, and our intellects can be stimulated. And we can see our emotions as good.

Steps to Take

1. Identify an emotional habit that you would like to change.
2. What events or thoughts trigger that feeling or habit?
3. How might you change the events that trigger the feeling?
4. What truth or Bible verse could you memorize to edit that feeling?
5. List the authorities in your life. Which one is most important to you?
6. How does your personal sense of worth reflect that authority?
7. You can place yourself directly under God's authority by reading the Bible regularly and allowing it to shape your conscience and behavior. Make a plan you can live with to include regular reading in your schedule.

> Remember the word to Thy servant,
> In which Thou hast made me hope.
> This is my comfort in my affliction,
> That Thy word has revived me.
> Thy statutes are my songs
> In the house of my pilgrimage.
> The LORD is my portion;
> I have promised to keep Thy words.
>
> Psalm 119:49-50, 54, 57